FIGHTING INFERTILITY

FIGHTING INFERTILITY

Finding My Inner Warrior Through Trying to
Conceive, IVF, and Miscarriage

SAMANTHA BUSCH

Health Communications, Inc.
Boca Raton, Florida

www.hcibooks.com

Library of Congress Cataloging-in-Publication Data
is available through the Library of Congress

© 2021 Samantha Busch

ISBN-13: 978-0-7573-2383-6 (Paperback)
ISBN-10: 0-7573-2383-9 (Paperback)
ISBN-13: 978-0-7573-2384-3 (ePub)
ISBN-10: 0-7573-2384-7 (ePub)

This book reflects the personal experiences of the author and is not meant to be a recommendation of any medical advice or treatment. Each reader should be guided by the advice of her medical advisor.

HCI, its logos, and marks are trademarks of Health Communications, Inc.

Publisher: Health Communications, Inc.
            1700 NW 2nd Ave.
            Boca Raton, FL 33432-1653

Cover photo taken by Olly Yung
Cover design by Larissa Hise Henoch
Interior design and formatting by Lawna Patterson Oldfield

To my husband, thank you for letting me talk about your sperm and our sex life to the world as casually as ordering fast food. I love you and cannot thank you enough for your love and your support during our crazy journey of trying to have children and writing a book. You are my true other half, the person who knows me best, my rock. I love doing life with you by my side and appreciate you every day.

Brexton, my heart bursts with how much I love you. You changed my world in the best possible way, and being your mother is the greatest gift from God. I am so proud and in awe of you as I watch you grow. I will always be your biggest fan, source of comfort, and fierce protector.

My girls, you both have changed me in the most fundamental ways, and I thank you for making me a stronger woman. You hold a piece of my heart in Heaven, and one day I will wrap you both in my arms and never let go.

To my mom, thank you for doing so many crossword puzzles over the years that you were able to come up with all the fancy words for my book. You are always my biggest supporter and best friend. No matter how old I get, I will always need you. With love and gratitude.

Thank you to the countless infertility warriors, many complete strangers, who at times were my biggest source of comfort when I felt most alone. You have given me the strength to find my voice to fight for this amazing community so that we are heard and understood, can forge a path for those to come, and can lift one another up. You are the strongest women I know!

Contents

Part I: OUR STORY

Part II: ADVICE

Part I

OUR STORY

1

LIFE COMES CRASHING TO A HALT

I was twenty-eight weeks pregnant when my husband crashed a racecar headfirst into a wall at the Daytona International Speedway.

That morning, I'd tried to roll over in the pitch blackness of our motorhome, my swollen, pregnant belly protesting at the motion. Momentarily disoriented, I knocked my glasses to the floor in a sleep-clumsy reach for the nightstand and tried to determine what it was that had woken me.

And then I heard it again, less than a minute later: a buzz, growing to a hum and finally a roar before slowly fading again to silence. Race engines. I remembered: we were at the Daytona International Speedway preparing for the first race weekend of the season. I must have slept late into the morning—*something I won't get to do too much longer,* I thought, as I felt the baby's first kicks of the day.

Our dog, Lucy, a tiny Pomeranian-Yorkie crossbreed, hopped up onto the pillow and started licking my face, excited for the day to start. Beside me, Kyle snored quietly, sleeping the kind of sleep only someone who *isn't* pregnant can enjoy. After kissing him sleepily on the cheek, I gently took his hand and placed it on my belly so he could wake to the baby's kicking too. He stirred, yawned, kissed *me* sleepily on the cheek, and opened the shades in our room. Light poured into the space, revealing a bright but overcast day in northeast Florida.

"Wow, we slept in for a change," he said. He was right—sleep was hard to come by lately as first-trimester morning sickness had been replaced by second-trimester insomnia. Most nights were spent catching a few minutes of sleep between endless hours of restless tossing and turning. I was glad to be starting this racing season fully rested for the first time in what felt like forever.

Slowly, we got out of bed and started our morning routines, and I wondered how different our mornings would soon become.

We sat across from each other at the dinette table and shared a healthy breakfast, with Kyle occasionally giving the swollen feet I placed in his lap a gentle rub between bites. Even though this would be my seventh year on the road with Kyle, I still got excited at the start of the season. I loved staying in our motorhome. It's a special place we designed together with incredible joy, from the paint and colors adorning the outside of the motorhome, which Kyle did, to my work on the interior, handpicking everything down to the stitching on the pillows. It was here that Kyle proposed to me, with one knee down on the just-right kitchen flooring we had chosen from hundreds of samples. This was a project we had painstakingly worked on together, and it felt like an extension of us. Spending time here is special, and we had built-in touches to make it even more so when the baby was born. The motorhome is bright and roomy and comfortable, with a modern feel and all the comforts of home. We already had a crib, which was currently being used as a pillow storage bin while waiting for the baby.

There was a built-in child safety gate tucked away for the future, and baby locks on all the drawers and cabinets. I had already stocked it with diapers, creams, pacifiers, toys, and clothes. I might have been nesting.

This time of togetherness was even more meaningful on that day—Daytona is always the first race of a new season, and we had big expectations for the months ahead. It was also the last time we would start a season without a child. We had worked so hard for this baby, spending years of our lives trying and failing to conceive. It felt like this day was the start of a new phase for us, and we took a moment together to take it all in. All that was missing was our son, who at that moment was happily squirming in my belly as I finished our breakfast.

After we ate, Kyle was off with his team, and I was ready to exercise. I popped barre class in the DVD player and gently stretched, noticing how much different it felt than before I was pregnant. As I rolled my yoga mat out over the hardwood floors, sweet hints of my now-wilting Valentine's flowers drifted across the room. With my feet squishing on the soft mat, I began to move. Exercising is my peaceful time, a personal place where I can be calm and centered and in the moment. During the racing season—nine months of nonstop travel and tracks every weekend, constantly being pulled in a million different directions—these moments matter. As I moved through the routine, I watched my growing belly in the mirrors decorating the room as they reflected how I felt: full, strong, and happy. Over the next several months, I often wished to come back to this moment. Before everything changed.

Walking onto the track was like the first day of school: seeing everyone again after a long off-season was exhilarating. Friends were congratulating me on the pregnancy, and I reveled in the attention. Kyle and I linked hands in prayer, joining the crowd in seeking safety and blessings for the season to come. It was a powerful moment, and as the National Anthem and flyover thundered through the track, contentment and pride surged in me. The baby, who had been kicking all morning, now slept quietly in the incredible noise of the massive arena, and Kyle's arm around the small of my back felt like home.

By the time I got to my seat in the pit box, the day had turned beautiful —warm, with just a hint of the ocean in the air over the smells of the track. I can't pretend it doesn't make me nervous seeing the man I love driving around a track at 200 miles per hour just fractions of an inch from other drivers. That morning, I knew it was possible to wreck. I had seen plenty of crashes, huge pileups, and vicious rollovers. Before every race, Kyle and I pray for his safety and the safety of other drivers, asking for divine intervention to ward off this fate.

While I had heard of serious injuries and even deaths occurring during races, even in the worst of the wrecks I had seen, the drivers always got out and walked away unharmed. There is so much thought and engineering that goes into safety in both the cars and the tracks that while I could imagine someone getting seriously hurt, it was hard to believe it would actually happen. So when I settled into the pit box and nestled the earpiece that lets me hear the radio traffic between Kyle, his spotter, and his team snugly into my ear, I held high hopes that even if a bad wreck did happen—something that is very common at Daytona—Kyle would be safe and sound, in the hands of an amazing team and a loving God.

Unless you have been to a race, you probably don't understand just how big the tracks are. In Daytona, cars scream down a straightaway that is more than a half-mile long at 200 miles per hour, disappearing almost as quickly as they come into view. In the blink of an eye, the small portion of track that is visible to us fills with cars and empties again. A wail that dwarfes the loudest thunder vibrates in your chest as the pack flies by and fades again until their next pass. When the cars were not in that small window, I checked Kyle's lap time tracker and the TV screen in front of me intently, liking what I saw. Kyle's spotter, Tony Hirschman, provided a calming commentary in my ear. He expertly guided Kyle through the pack, telling him to go high or low, warning him of drivers to watch out for, and setting him up for a win to start the season. It was going so smoothly, and so comfortably, that it took a moment to register what happened when Kyle wrecked.

The first hint I had of something going wrong was Tony's worried voice over the radio as he tried to guide Kyle through the pack. It was nearing the end of the race, and with a few laps left Kyle was in fifth place. Tony was setting Kyle up to push his teammate into the lead and let the two of them duke it out for the win.

And that's when it happened.

"Go high, Kyle. Now! Get up higher."

Kyle's teammate began to spin out in the pack, careening off other cars, sending the pack scattering in every direction.

I didn't know it then, but Kyle was hurtling over the infield grass. All I heard was Tony giving frantic directions in my ear:

"Hit the brakes, Kyle. Lock it down. Lock it down now!"

And then, in a tone of voice I had never heard from Tony before, he asked, "Kyle, are you okay?"

As the spotter, Tony is perched at the highest point above the track and is the only person on the team who can see everything. Helpless to prevent it, he would have seen what I could not: Kyle speeding off the track, across a field of grass, brakes not working, and then his car slamming headfirst into the wall—the unprotected infield wall, with no SAFER barrier to absorb the impact. Tony would have seen the flames erupt from the engine and the sinister puff of black smoke that followed. But with the way his voice sounded in my ear, I knew it wasn't good even without seeing what happened.

There was no answer from my husband.

"Are you okay, Kyle?"

When Kyle and I started dating, I made only one unbreakable rule about racing: if he wrecks, he must get on the radio right away to let me know he's okay, no matter what.

That day, he broke his promise.

I've never experienced such silence at a racetrack. I knew cars were still on the track, engines revving around me, drivers impatient to get back into the race after having been stopped for the wreck. The cheering and noise from the crowd could not penetrate the burning silence from Kyle's end of the radio.

"Kyle, talk to me. Are you okay?" In Tony's voice there was a tightness I had never heard from him before. He sounded afraid.

And still nothing from Kyle. Fear sat cold in the pit of my stomach next to the baby growing there. I looked around, desperately trying to see Kyle. If I could just see him, I would know he was all right.

But I couldn't see him. I could see the faces of the crew in the pit box, though, and the breathless horror in their eyes filled me with dread. I started to pray, my heart pounding out of my chest and my life unraveling in my imagination. Except, with time stretching out and Kyle still silent, it wasn't imaginary.

Something was terribly wrong.

And that was it; I wasn't going to wait another second. I jumped out of the box and started to move as quickly as I could to the infield care center where injured drivers are always tended to. Along the way, a cameraman told me that Kyle was getting out of the car. For a moment, my fear eased, that icy knot loosening and warming. I looked back over my shoulder, that moment caught on camera for the national broadcast. I thanked him and got back on the move. For a moment, I thought Kyle was okay.

For a moment.

When I arrived at the infield care center, I was left alone in a room with PR staff from our team and Kerby, our motorhome driver. Nobody would look me in the eye, and nobody could get me answers. I begged Kerby to find me some information, anything at all, but he was as helpless as I was, stranded in a room with nothing but horrible questions. I couldn't understand why we were still waiting—Kyle should have been in the medical area by now, and I should have been with him, holding his hand as he was checked out by the medical staff and sent on his way with a clean bill of health.

Finally, after the longest minutes in the history of the world, a grim-faced NASCAR nurse came in and told me I needed to get to the hospital immediately. I asked her for any information at all. Her only response was to hug me and whisper in my ear that I needed to go now while I cried into her shoulder.

I don't remember getting into the car. I don't remember who drove me. I got in, and I went to the hospital, not knowing if Kyle would be alive when I got there. It was only a few miles from the track, and we broke every traffic law in Florida to get there quickly, but it was the longest ride of my life. I remember thinking we shouldn't be speeding like this with a pregnant woman in the car, yet thinking we needed to drive so much faster.

It was not supposed to be like this. I placed my hand on my belly, over the baby we worked so hard to conceive, and I cried, mascara streaking down my cheeks and making small black blots on the white lapels of my blazer where the tears fell.

Ours was the story of making this baby *together*. Through tears and shots and struggle and years of uncertainty, failed pregnancy tests and shattered dreams, we faced each step together. He was my rock, and I was terrified that he was now crumbling. This couldn't become a story of me raising this child alone.

We arrived at the hospital. I steeled myself for what was to come and stepped out of the car. I needed Kyle, but today, Kyle needed me more. It was my turn to be the rock.

2

DESTINED TO BE

The day I met Kyle was the first day I had ever been to a racetrack. It was 2007, and I was going into my senior year at Purdue, finishing my psychology degree. I grew up in a family of modest means outside Chicago, which meant I worked my way through college, mostly as a waitress, fitness instructor, and promotional model.

In my work as a model, I was hired by brands to demonstrate products at trade shows and conventions, and sometimes at larger events. This time, my work took me to the VIP area at the Indianapolis Motor Speedway, where select sponsors and fans could take a ride around the track. I happily chatted with people while they waited their turn, helping the event staff check IDs and talking with friendly strangers from around the country about my time at Purdue. It was brutally hot, at least 100°F with nearly 100 percent humidity. My black shorts and black tee clung to my body, drawing in more heat—and maybe attracting more than just the sun. As the line dwindled, a kind blonde woman with a branded polo shirt and laminated credentials asked me if I would like a ride. In that moment, all I could think of was air conditioning and immediately accepted.

"Oh, that AC feels so good," I exclaimed as I settled into the seat of the street-ready car.

The driver glanced over and slowly looked me up and down. He was wearing a black shirt similar to mine, even adorned with the same sponsor's logo, and reflective sunglasses. With a rakish half smile, he asked, "Are you ready?" Almost before I could respond, he took off.

As he drove, we started talking. He asked me my name and other basic questions about me. He was interesting and interested, and even though he was a little shy, I was enjoying our conversation. And to be fair, I looked good. I had on bright red lip gloss, and even with the heat, I made that sponsor's fitted shirt look as fashionable as possible, with a lot of summer-tanned leg showing beneath black shorts. My normally wavy hair had been transformed by the humidity into a waterfall of brunette curls cascading down my back, and I was feeling it. I guess the driver noticed.

Now, I know we were driving fast. I know that a couple of laps around the track is a very quick blip of time, but I never noticed the stands flying by or the incline of the track, or how gravity pulled me from side to side as we rocketed around the turns. It was exciting, but it was because of the driver and not because of the drive. He seemed sweet, so I invited him out with me and my girlfriends later in the night. I wasn't sure if it was the speed, or the setting, or him, but I was feeling sparks. Except he said no. He had other plans, he said, and I guessed I had misread the situation.

After the ride, I was finishing up my duties when the same nice woman with the laminated credentials who'd sent me on the ride came along and asked me for my number, which was unusual. I wasn't sure what to think—I was *just* talking to him—and didn't know why he didn't ask me himself. I gave her my number, thinking maybe he was shy.

After the race, I went to a friend's house where I received a text from him asking if I liked the ride. Texting was still pretty rare and not easy to do on the old flip phones, and a huge grin spread across my face. As my friend and I shared a snack, I told her the story of what happened. Her father, who happened to be a big NASCAR fan, overheard and started giving me the third degree.

"Where exactly were you? Tell it again. What happened?"

I told the story again.

"What was his name?" he asked excitedly.

"Kyle," I said.

"What's his last name?"

I didn't know. He was just some guy whose job it was to give VIPs a thrill ride. I never asked his last name.

What my friend's father knew that I didn't was that actual NASCAR drivers handled those duties. In a few seconds, he pulled up Google on his computer and typed in "Kyle Busch."

"Is this him?"

On the screen, Kyle smiled back at me. A little cocky, a little sweet. It was him, for sure, I said.

"He's kind of a big deal," he responded.

When I found out what Kyle did for a living, it was a bit of a turnoff at first. Not that he was a NASCAR driver, but that he was a professional athlete. If the frat boys I dated at Purdue were immature, what would a bad-boy racer nicknamed "Rowdy" be like?

Kyle asked me to the race. I declined because I had to work. He asked me out more than once. I continued to decline. Not because of Kyle—but because of where my life was headed. I was juggling school and four jobs, and adding a romantic entanglement onto my plate that I didn't know was heading anywhere was not in the master plan. But he persisted over the next few weeks, taking the time to get to know me and not demanding that I meet him on his terms. He was sweet, and kind, and *interesting*.

And so, I began a courtship with up-and-coming racecar driver Kyle Busch.

Dating Kyle was both thoroughly modern and a bit old-fashioned. His life kept him on the road. Mine kept me firmly in place at Purdue. This was 2007, and social media wasn't much to speak of yet. It seems so dated today, but the only real way to communicate was for us to talk on the phone, and so we did.

A lot.

It started kind of slowly. At first, I found myself checking my phone more often, hoping a text would pop through, or sending him one occasionally. Nothing big—just a "Good luck on your race," from me; a "How did the test go?" from him. Soon, I found myself watching my first race as I was working out at the gym, and immediately texted him to let him know. Before long it was quick calls. Then it was long calls.

In fact, we talked for more than four months before I finally agreed to go on a date.

There is an intimacy you can achieve with that level of conversation over such a long time that just doesn't happen in college life. Most of us met guys at booze-filled parties. In those relationships, you develop a physical intimacy before an emotional one—and so often the emotional connection never develops.

That's okay. That's how people learn, and not every connection needs to be soul changing.

For us, it was different. It was late nights with my hair up and PJ pants on, talking on the phone. I'd hear my friends outside my small bedroom getting ready for a weeknight party that I was suddenly skipping to talk to Kyle. I'd hear music blaring from the downstairs apartment, hooting and hollering in the party as the smells of nearby restaurants I wasn't visiting wafted through my open window. These were all things I used to be part of, but they seemed less important the closer Kyle and I became. We had our first dates hundreds or thousands of miles apart, him alone in his bus, me in my room, snuggled under covers. We would talk until the batteries died.

It's not to say that I knew at any point during this time that Kyle and I were destined for more. His life was *vastly different* from mine. Months and months on the road, press and fans, and a shining spotlight always turned on. I didn't know if that was compatible with what I wanted, if we could make our lives mesh. I was in an elite psychology program with only ten other students. I was set to graduate at the top of my class. I was making plans for grad school, I was almost certain to be accepted into the program of my dreams, and I had a plan for my life. None of the possibilities that lay before me and Kyle had ever been part of that plan.

What I did know was that I was getting to know him in a way I hadn't previously come to know other men, and I liked it.

I liked *him*.

I admired the way he talked about racing and his determination to be the best at it. He was committed to breaking records, to becoming the best driver in the history of the sport. We had that in common—we both were driven to achieve the very most we could.

We didn't have racing in common, though, and it led to some interesting misunderstandings. I remember him emailing me about having to test Loudon, a racetrack in New Hampshire that I never knew existed. Later on the phone, I politely told him London had an *n* and not a *u*. I presumed testing was some kind of driving test and asked him how he studied for it. When he finished laughing, he explained it meant trying out the track. Slowly, we learned each other's language.

It was after one particularly long conversation—two and a half hours in the middle of the night that passed in the blink of an eye—I thought Kyle and I might have something more. We talked about everything. Dating in college had been a string of college boys. They wanted sex and to talk about themselves. Kyle was different—maybe it was the distance, the elimination of sex from the equation, but he *listened*. He asked questions. He wanted to know about me.

And he talked about his dogs.

There was something about the way Kyle described his pets that won me over. He had such obvious love and devotion to these animals. It was so unexpected: This tough, stoic racecar driver became a marshmallow when he talked about his dogs. I saw the kind of love Kyle had inside him. I saw that he wasn't afraid to talk about that kind of love, to be open. To connect.

I *really* liked him.

Finally, in the fall, Kyle and I agreed to spend a weekend together. This was no easy task, given that he was in a different city every weekend and I was in Indiana, but eventually I flew to Texas to see what we might have. I refused to let him buy my ticket—I didn't want money clouding our relationship. He argued, but I won.

I spent hours packing for that trip, carefully folding outfits only to pull them out and try something different. While I didn't want there to be pressure, there was *significance* to this meeting. Could sustaining what we'd had over the phone work in person? Or was this going to be a bust? I was so excited to see Kyle, but I was also worried that I had built him into something he wasn't. It's easy to be one way on the phone and another in person, and seventy-two hours is a *long* first date.

He picked me up at the airport, and I was about as nervous as I'd ever been. I'd dated a lot in college, but I'd never been on a date with someone I already knew like I knew Kyle. Would what was special about us go away once the distance disappeared?

When we arrived at the restaurant for dinner, it turned out to be my worries that disappeared. We were seated at a booth. The hostess put our menus on the table across from one another like most people sit. Kyle remained standing as I slipped into the booth, picked up his menu, looked me right in the eye, and sat down next to me. It was sweet and unexpected and made me feel instantly that things with him were going to be different.

It was during the season, so Kyle was living in his motorhome. He used this word often, but I didn't have a sense of exactly what it was. When we arrived, I was shocked to discover there was only one bed.

Up until this point, the date had been going well—lots of affectionate touches and good meshing of our personalities, and so much laughter filled the night. So, when this single-bed situation arose, it seemed presumptuous, and I was a little taken aback. I had certainly had my share of flings, but this felt deeper—more of a connection, and I wanted the physical part of our relationship to share some of the special slow building of our emotional relationship. In a huff, I stuffed a big pillow between the two of us and we went to sleep. Well, if you can call lying awake analyzing every detail of our date sleeping, that is.

I didn't want physicality coming between what we had, and I was put out that it seemed like he presumed we'd be sleeping together. But he was a perfect gentleman and never did anything to make me feel rushed or uncomfortable. Once I came to understand that, it made it easy to be in the same place as him. We continued in person as we had over the phone, and it was wonderful to see his facial expressions and his gestures and his interest in what I had to say.

One of the lucky similarities of my life as a student and his life as a race-car driver was that we both had scheduled downtime around the holidays. Over my Christmas break that year, Kyle surprised me with a vacation. Because I didn't know where we were going (Kyle refused to tell anyone except my parents), I packed for every different climate. Cute boots went into the suitcase next to even cuter bikinis. I packed a little black dress and a long black jacket, and a *lot* of makeup—and maybe just a little bit of special lingerie as my little Christmas present to Kyle. I begged my mom and dad to give me a clue as to where we were headed. They didn't budge.

I packed my bulging bags into Kyle's car, and we headed to the airport. I asked to see the tickets. He declined. I tried to sneak a peek at check-in, but he told the ticket agents the trip was a surprise. It wasn't until we finally reached the gate that I saw where we were going, and I just about died. It was perfect—switching the cold Chicago winter for the sun and sand of the Cayman Islands.

Those four days were among the best of my life. Finally, Kyle and I were able to add a physical presence to our emotional relationship. We had a beautiful room that looked out over the ocean, and all day and night the everchanging Caribbean was our constant companion. Waves rolled in and out beneath the smell of tropical flowers and the songs of island birds. We slept in. We talked for hours, the adventure of lying alone under new-to-me stars opened us up to one another in new-to-me ways. We could hold hands and see facial expressions and breathe the same air in the same place. Leaving Kyle at the end of the trip was harder than leaving the island, and leaving the island was *hard*. I cried at the airport, in direct contradiction to what I knew about myself; I didn't want anything serious. I didn't want to blow up my life.

Falling in love was *not* in my plans.

There was the matter of distance and our lives: When I returned to Purdue, he went back on the road. We were not solidified in our relationship, and I didn't know if we could be. I went through classes, I worked, and I continued to progress toward the educational goals I was so close to achieving. I went to parties and lived it up with my friends, knowing that college was soon coming to an end, and a life with more responsibilities was about to start. But mostly, I thought about Kyle. I looked forward to his calls more and more, and during the time we spent talking, all the other things slowly disappeared.

May came, and I graduated.

It was time to decide.

Throughout college, I planned to go to graduate school and pursue a master's degree in industrial and organizational psychology. From a young age, my parents instilled the idea that education was important, but so was my future—and if Kyle was my future, I knew that our relationship could not survive another three years apart while I was in school.

I won't pretend it wasn't agonizing. I had acceptance letters sitting on my desk, and I was torn in two every time Kyle's name flashed on the display of my phone. I worried a *lot* about losing my identity as anything more than "Kyle's girlfriend." I didn't want to disappoint my parents or leave the friendships I'd built while at Purdue. I wanted to be my own person. Which of course was what Kyle wanted for me, but in the end for that to happen together, we would have to *be* together.

And so, just like I did when I strapped myself into that car for a ride over a year ago, I jumped into the unknown.

I chose Kyle. I was moving to Charlotte.

3

ALL ROADS LEAD TO NEW BEGINNINGS

The loud "scrrrtch" of the packing tape unrolling for the last time echoed in my empty bedroom. My mother held the final box closed as I carefully smoothed a final clear strip over the flaps, sealing away the last of the life I had always known. When I looked up, the tears in her eyes were obscured by the tears in mine.

Throughout my life, my parents had helped me with every move, building beds and painting walls and secondhand furniture and so much cleaning. They had always been there without complaint, just wanting to see me safe and happy. But this time was different.

Now I would not be a quick hour-and-a-half away, able to sneak home on weekends when I just needed my own bed and the comfort of Mom's Sunday gravy. Nor could my dad just pop in when his work "brought him out that way," lingering over a shared lunch and his familiar, comfortable laugh. I couldn't make a special trip home to help my little brother with a school project.

To say I was apprehensive was an understatement.

I grew up in northwest Indiana, just outside Chicago where so many people I loved still lived. Most of my family was less than an hour's drive away. My little brother, Steven, was still in school, and I cherished my role as a big sister. We're a close-knit family where aunts and uncles and cousins —and even second and third cousins—all regularly got together for huge family parties and summer barbecues, holidays and birthdays, and just-because celebrations that meant the world to me. Most of the kids I grew up with went to Purdue with me or to nearby schools, and we'd remained close.

Moving away from them felt like moving away from an important part of myself.

The weeks before the move, as I began to pack and sort and filter through the detritus of my childhood, were like a nostalgia parade. Old friends came to wish me well and say goodbye. Close girlfriends came by to return long-borrowed clothing and share the last in-person laughs for a while. I did so much hugging that my arms were sore. Each visit carried memories with it—cheer practice or sleepovers or getting ready for first dates, giggling and learning how to put on makeup, crying and consoling one another over pints of ice cream when those dates turned out to be the special kind of jerks only boys in high school can be.

So, when I looked up and saw my mom tearing up, I couldn't help myself. I started crying too. Neither of us could believe this was happening. Don't get me wrong, I was also happy and excited to be starting this new part of my life with Kyle, but in that moment, it hit me that I was going to mourn what I was saying goodbye to. So many people I loved would be going through their day-to-day lives, and I wouldn't be there. I would be a distant ghost, passing through hazy imaginings of a life I couldn't truly be a part of anymore.

I felt overwhelmed by sadness.

But it was time. Steven came in, saw me and Mom hugging it out over tears, and silently picked up the last box to load it into the car. I did not know it at the time, but he tucked a little letter inside the tape to tell me how much he was going to miss me. I still read that letter to this day, and it still brings me back to that moment of intense emotions twisting around me.

Suddenly it was time. Pops, my dad, held my hand as we walked to the car, and he gave me the biggest bear hug before I got in the driver's seat. I remember the prickle of his goatee against my cheek, and the catch in his voice, thick as molasses with emotion, as he told me he loved me, begged me to drive safe, and reminded me he could always drive down with a shotgun if Kyle ever hurt me.

Next it was Mom's turn. I have never hugged anyone longer than I hugged her right then, standing outside on the driveway in the warm sun of an Indiana summer. I don't even know what we said to each other. I was just soaking up each second of her presence, of her love, and trying to push as much of my love back to her. Finally, she pulled away and nodded at me with a smile.

It was okay. I could go.

And I did. I got in the car, which was hot and sticky already, and started the engine. As I rolled down the windows until the AC could catch up, my heart was pounding in my chest, and I felt a little like I was going to throw up. But I did it. I did the hardest thing I've ever done, and left my parents. The only life I had known receded in the rearview mirror. I saw Pops waving and then wipe his eyes as I turned the corner.

Once I was sure I was out of sight, I pulled over to the side of the road and had a good, long cry. The whole time, I fought the urge to turn the car around and drive back home. Just then, my phone dinged—it was a text from Kyle.

"Drive safe, Babe. Can't wait until you get home."

"Home." It was the first time I had thought of Charlotte and the house where Kyle lived as my home. It was a fresh breeze, carrying the worst of my sadness away with it. I cried out the last of the tears, took a deep breath, put the car in gear, and hit the road, heading toward my future.

The first few months in North Carolina were a mix of great happiness, incredible excitement, and a bit of sadness. Kyle's home was beautiful, with a lush yard and a bright blue pool. Kyle made sure to help turn *his* home into *our* home.

We painted together, adding artwork and decorations and soft feminine touches to counterbalance the bachelor vibe that existed before I arrived. He introduced me to his friends on the racing circuit, several of whom had young wives or girlfriends in situations just like mine. I began to build new friendships—but it wasn't the same. I missed my family back home, and I missed the friends with whom I had developed the shorthand of lifelong relationships, people who could read my face the way Kyle could read a racetrack. I missed inside jokes and familiar restaurants and the easy comfort of knowing someone was close by even if you didn't see them every day.

It did not help that Kyle's work often kept him away from home. I spent days at a time alone, and I might not see a single other person in those days. Gone were the days of simply walking next door in my apartment complex to a living room strewn with people and books. I missed the ease of sending a text to meet a girlfriend to go for a long walk around campus. Now, I found myself alone in a strange town with only a handful of acquaintances, none of whom I felt comfortable enough with yet even to invite out to lunch.

This was during the racing season, so I also had to get used to life on the road, just as I was getting used to life in my new home.

One thing that surprised me was that despite all these changes, I was bored. These long stretches of time alone left me with little to do but think, and I'm a person who needs to be occupied. I need to be working toward goals and moving forward, so I enrolled in an online master's degree program at Austin Peay State University in industrial and organizational psychology. It felt good to be using my brain again, but I still missed my friends, my family, and my old life.

I remember one night on the phone with my girlfriend Bre. I was at home, tidying up and putting away laundry while she was back on campus getting ready to go out to our favorite bar.

"Oh, you should be here," she said, and I agreed. I could hear music blaring in the background, and laughter.

"Tell me what's been happening!" I leaned back into the kitchen counter and looked at the laundry basket, willing the clothes to fold themselves. They didn't. Behind Bre, the sound of laughter and activity got louder and closer to the phone. I heard her squeal with laughter.

"Sorry, Sam, gotta go! I'll call you soon!"

And then she was gone.

I texted my mom. She was out with my aunts and not able to talk. "We all send our love," she texted. I reached out to friend after friend after friend from home, but they were all out living their lives—lives I used to live with them.

Those first weeks in Charlotte were filled with loneliness. And I thought about it for a while, looking at this beautiful home I found myself in. I thought about the charmed life Kyle and I had—and the fact that I got to share it with him. I thought of all the good things I had in my life, and imagined the future stretching out before me. I saw the house full of kids, toys underfoot, and the perfect sound of babies laughing. I saw Kyle with his hair running to salt and pepper, coming home from work and putting his arms around my waist. I looked in the backyard and saw it full of new friends and old coming together for parties and barbecues.

Slowly, I found myself. As we traveled, I left the motorhome and went out to explore cities on my own. I invited new friends and did the hard work of building meaningful relationships with them. And through it all, I kept in touch with the people I loved back home. I realized I didn't have to let go of them, I just had to hold on to them a little less tightly, and suddenly I could breathe again.

As this was happening, Kyle and I did the hard work of building a relationship. I'm not going to lie; it wasn't always easy. Going from a long-distance relationship to one where you are in the same space brings a huge set of challenges. We definitely got on each other's nerves from time to time. We had to learn how to live with each other as well as we loved each other.

But we did. We found patience—not our best quality—and under-standing, and started living a shared life. We figured out how to read each other's moods, when it was okay to ask for space and when to jump into something. That first year was overwhelming, but there was so much growth, and so much love.

And at the end of it, by leaving my old life behind, I found a new life to love.

4

ENGAGING

We had found our groove and were living life in the fast lane. In our first years together, Kyle was racking up wins and breaking records on the track, and I felt like I was racking up my own wins in life. Our charitable foundation was expanding, and my passion for philanthropic work was growing along with it. Kyle and I founded a race team together, and we built a huge race shop to go with it.

All along, we did everything together. When we needed to design the shop, we stayed up late in the night picking out just the right look and branding. We were traveling nonstop, making media appearances, building new friendships with other racing couples, and living our lives to the fullest. I also spent time building a lifestyle blog, giving me a way to connect with women who would soon become so important in my life. It was a whirlwind, spinning this way and that, always busy with a never-ending series of demands, but it never *felt* that way because Kyle and I were managing it together. In every sense of the word we were a team, learning how to support each other as we learned how to do all of the other things we were doing.

Like building our motorhome.

Motorhomes make life much more manageable for drivers and their families. Racing families spend so much time on the road, and so much time at the tracks, that it's very difficult to make it work with flying and hotels. The motorhome gives us a place that is ours for the many months of the year we spend on the road. And when I met Kyle? Well, let's just say his motorhome wasn't meant to be shared with a woman.

It was full of multicolored lighting and video game systems. It had no decor, just a lot of stuff. There were no soft touches, there were no visual comforts. It was a bachelor pad on wheels.

That was *not* going to cut it for the both of us, and to his credit, Kyle knew that.

We spent months building our own motorhome together. For both of us, for our future, and it was so much fun. Literally from the floorboards up, this was an expression of the both of us. We looked at flooring and walls and tiles and fixtures and decor, and we designed each little bit as something that would feel like a place where we both wanted to live.

That's not to say there were no disagreements at all. I mean, who the heck needs a TV in the shower? (Hint: Kyle does.) But even those were small and manageable, things we figured out as part of the same team trying to achieve the same thing. None of it was overwhelming. None of it felt contentious. It just felt like everything else we did together: just right.

Our first night together in the finished motorhome was at the Daytona International Speedway in 2010. Kyle was at the track for a qualifying event, and I was sitting in the motorhome with one eye on the TV while typing up a recipe for the blog. After a quick dinner, I decided to start getting ready for bed.

Stepping into the bathroom, I turned on the water, waited for it to warm, and started splashing it on my face. It was just then that the door banged open and I heard Kyle step inside.

"What are you doing?" Short, almost abrupt. It seemed unusual.

"I think it's pretty obvious," I replied through a soft white terrycloth towel as I dried the last of the water off my face.

"Do you still have your eyes in?" he asked excitedly.

"What?"

"Your eyes! Do you still have them in?"

"Yeah, why?" I did still have my contacts in, but even without them I could have worn my glasses. I had no idea what this was about.

He darted into the bathroom, took me by the hand, and pulled me into the living room. The new floors were cool under my feet, unfamiliar and yet as comfortable as home in our new space.

He took me into his arms and held me close.

"Do you love our new home?" he whispered into my ear.

"Of course, I do," I replied. "It's perfect."

He went on to gush about the space. The little flourishes we picked out together, and how every piece had some of each of us in it. He talked about the walls and the trim and even the custom headboard, and how much he loved all of it.

"Are you thinking about switching to a career in interior design?" I laughed. I mean, I knew he liked the place, but I didn't know he had even noticed some of the minutiae.

"Nope. I just love that we built it together. I've loved everything we've built together. In fact, there's nothing we can't build together. We're the perfect team. There's nothing in this world that makes me happier than making you happy. And I'm happier than I've ever been in my life when I'm with you."

My normally reserved boyfriend was suddenly being sappy? I didn't know what to make of it. Until suddenly he was down on one knee, a small, black velvet box in his hand. Tears leapt to my eyes. Was this really happening? I stopped breathing and heard nothing but the pounding of my heart in my ears. My mind flashed back to memories of our long phone calls from Purdue, our first kiss, the tender moments in each other's arms, and now the man was down on his knee before me. I knew he was the one—I'd known for quite some time. But the season was starting tomorrow! We had just started our race team! We had so much to do!

And then the sound of his voice rushed me back to the moment, and I heard him ask, "Samantha, will you marry me?"

I half tackled him to the floor, tears and kisses flying. He laughed and pulled back for a moment, breathless.

"So, is that a yes?"

"Of course, it's a yes!" I squealed and started kissing him some more.

In what was becoming a life of perfect moments, this was the most perfect one of them all. We were getting married.

5

PLANNED TO PERFECTION

The next morning, Kyle was back at work, and so was I—planning our wedding. You've probably figured out that I dive into a planning project wholeheartedly. If you thought planning the motorhome was bad, well, the wedding was a whole new level.

A few hours later, Kyle found me sitting on the same floor he proposed to me on the night before, surrounded by an explosion of magazine clippings. Dresses and place settings and bouquets and invitation ideas were on one side, locations and vows and reception ideas the other, and everything else you could think of surrounded me in hastily arranged piles.

Kyle's eyes widened. "So, you've been busy," was all he said, eyeing the magazine cutouts covering every spare inch of the motorhome.

"I can't help it! I was so surprised, and now I've got to make up for lost time!"

I started to show him what I'd been working on. Pictures of cloud-like canopies of pure-white flowers suspended over the heads of seated bridal parties. The most exotic and secluded honeymoon destinations, veils and trains covered in lace vows that made me cry just trying to read them all the way through. My excitement must have been contagious because soon he was as deep down the rabbit hole as I was, on his knees sorting through pictures putting them in "yes," "no," and "maybe" piles.

We started talking about wedding dates.

"Well, your schedule doesn't leave a lot of room," I said.

"That's true," he agreed.

"I mean, we could get married on Easter. A spring wedding would be beautiful and perfect for fresh flowers. Really, it would take a miracle to get a wedding this size together that quickly. But much later and we're into the sweltering heat of summer. We don't want that!"

"What about winter?" he asked.

"Winter?" My jaw dropped. "Really? Winter? I can't believe you'd even say that! You know it's cold in winter and that I hate the cold!"

"Well, unless we get married on a Tuesday, I don't have a heck of a lot of downtime that isn't in the winter." He had a point.

"But do you really want our wedding guests to be bundled up in heavy coats and boots and mittens and gloves? Do you want them battling snow-storms and icy roads and having to deal with canceled flights? I mean, my wedding dress will be about as revealing as a ski suit if we get married in winter. Do you want to marry a woman wearing a ski suit?" I tapped my foot on the floor.

"Just hear me out," he pleaded, desperate to get back on track. "New Year's Eve."

All my life, I knew I wanted to get married at the Holy Name Cathedral in Chicago. I walked past it many times as a little girl when my mom and

Grandma would take me for a day in the city, and I dreamed of passing through its enormous doorway in my wedding dress, with the warm spring sun shining down on my bare shoulders. Then I pictured it in late December, in January. I really tried to picture it, and I came back to the snowsuit.

"Kyle, do you remember Chicago in December? It's so *cold*."

"It's not just December. It's New Year's Eve—it's an anniversary I could never forget, and besides, I am never cold when I'm with you."

Okay. I melted a little. Suddenly, I could see it. Christmas lights would still be up around the city. The love and optimism that always fill the world as one year ends and a new year begins would all be part of our wedding. Images of guests sipping champagne from glasses that matched crystal chandeliers hanging from ornate ceilings filled my mind, and the idea of ending one chapter of our lives and starting a new one just as a fresh, new year came to be? It felt right.

I decided I loved it, and like I had the night before, I jumped on Kyle and covered him in kisses. He laughed, and I shooed him out of the motorhome and back to work. With a happy sigh I picked up the pile of spring wedding fashions and floral arrangements and dumped them into the trash. I had ten months to plan the perfect wedding—time to get to work.

Ten months is not a lot of time to plan such an event, and the details were agonizing. We tried to pick a theme, spent hour after hour looking through fashion and wedding magazines, browsing the Web, and looking through other materials on our quest for the perfect place. Winter Wonderland felt done. A *Great Gatsby* theme felt a little contrived. When we took a break from themes, we looked at decor. Vases and linens and table settings and place cards and chair covers and soon our eyes were glazing over. We just couldn't make a decision to save our lives, and we were already out of time. Most of the venues we were looking at book years in advance.

Susan, the best wedding planner in Chicago, reminded us that our difficulty making a decision was because we hadn't picked a theme yet, and that once we did, everything would fall into place. Knowing she was right, we planned a trip to Chicago to look at reception venues and see some of these things in person that we had been struggling with. It was the best idea we'd had.

Why was it such a good idea? First, it let me bring my parents into the process. They are such great support and always have smart ideas. Second, seeing things on a screen and seeing them in person are two vastly different things. The four of us, along with Susan, toured the Field Museum, the Chicago Theater, trendy warehouses in the art district, sleek modern rooftops overlooking the city, and so many other places. We loved them all, but none felt right for our reception.

So, Susan suggested we visit her warehouse and start to look in on decor to see if any new inspiration struck. By this point, my dad and Kyle were both looking like they just wanted us to go to the City Clerk's office and get it over with, so we sent them to a bar to watch a game while Mom and I browsed.

As Mom and I sat in a big warehouse with Susan and a team of designers with each one voicing a different theme and opinion, I felt overwhelmed. The large room was overflowing with tables, chairs, linens, vases, crystals, and candles in every shape and style. Staff members ushered us around and showed us their favorite designs and tablescapes, spinning stories of how luxurious or elegant or daring or modern our wedding could be, and still nothing felt like the one. Each unique layout was stunning, but needing a moment to gather our thoughts, Mom and I asked if we could wander on our own and see what spoke to us. Seeing the panic bubbling behind my eyes, Susan quickly agreed, and we left the showroom to meander up and down the long aisles of her warehouse.

As we strolled, I asked about my mother's and grandmother's weddings. Although suffering from severe dementia in her later years, my grandmother had always had an outsized and sparkling personality. In her day, she would have loved doing this with us, picking out everything glam and glitzy from the warehouse. From time to time, we'd stop and pick something that seemed special off the shelf and carry it along with us, imagining what Grandma would think. Eventually, we made our way back to the showroom and laid out the pieces we'd picked on a long, white-covered table: feathers and baubles, bright and shining and full of Grandma.

In an instant, the theme hit us. The whole wedding would be an ode to her—a vintage glam wedding, with dark plums, deep reds, golds, rich, and velvety textures complemented by crystals and long colorful feathers of peacock and ostrich. It was right up her alley, and I loved knowing we could make her unique personality part of our day.

I called Kyle in an excited triumph.

"Hello?" His voice was nearly washed out over my dad's hooting and hollering at whatever game happened to be on the TV. In a rush, I told him about everything we had decided, and he was just as excited as I was. It really did suit us just right.

Susan announced she had just the right place for our reception. I told Kyle the address and asked him to meet us there.

The Chicago Cultural Center was built in the late 1800s as the city's first public library. It was designed to show the world that Chicago was a true modern metropolis, and no expense was spared in its construction. Exotic imported marble adorns the interior, and beautiful fixtures and accents of bronze create an air of elegance and majesty. Lush hardwood polished until it nearly glows fills the space, connecting past and present. But the truly special thing, the part that sets this nineteenth-century gem apart from anywhere else in the world, is the stunning Tiffany stained-glass dome that is set into the stone ceiling.

At thirty-eight feet across, with more than thirty thousand individual pieces of handcrafted glass, the stained-glass dome is the world's largest, and it is magnificent. As we stood beneath it, a rainbow of colors burst through, bathing us in multicolored light, and we knew it was the place.

When Kyle kissed me beneath the ornate dome, I could envision our first dance in this very spot as husband and wife, and I was even more sure.

While there were still months to go, making this decision felt like the hard work was done. The summer and autumn passed, and the rest of the details fell into place. I picked my wedding party, helped design my dress, and did it all in the middle of the craziness of the racing season. Before we knew it, the winter was upon us—and so was our wedding day.

6

WHEN TWO BECOME ONE

The big day was finally here. Even the weather seemed to lean into our future. Winter in Chicago is blustery and cold, with hard, frigid wind off the lake blowing huge drifts of snow into every corner, but not for us. On this day, it was like Mother Nature herself was my matron of honor. Even though it was overcast, the temperatures were nearly a record high for the city in midwinter, with calm winds and a sense of peace settling in over the Windy City. The glorious weather seemed to reinforce the fairy-tale life I was living—not even Chicago's winter could change our happy ending.

Inside our two-floor suite at the downtown Westin, my wedding party felt like the curtain had just gone up on a Broadway production. Waitstaff fairly danced in with carts of delicious finger foods as the women I loved surrounded me in front of the mirrors. Hairstylists pirouetted as makeup artists waved their brushes and wands like conductors, helping us all get ready for my big day. I felt like a queen sitting on her throne as a hair stylist crafted a masterpiece out of my brunette locks—a larger-than-life updo with all of the bobby pins in Chicago and clip-on extensions expertly woven into a work of art atop my head. The smell of mimosas, hairspray, powder, and flowery perfumes gave the room an almost tropical aroma, and we chatted and gossiped, laughing about my upcoming wedding night and the baby they all thought would be following nine months later. While I was certainly no virgin, butterflies filled my stomach as I imagined making love to my *husband* on the soft white sheets. I might have blushed a bit, making everyone laugh harder.

Susan came in carrying an envelope and a beautiful gift bag.

"It's from Kyle," she gushed. "You've got yourself a special one there."

All of the women let out a collective "aww," and I started blushing again with delight. They prodded me to read it aloud to the group, but I wanted this to be a private moment—the closest I'd get to being with Kyle before we were at the altar. I leapt out of my chair and ran upstairs to the bedroom, where I slept alone the night before in keeping with tradition. Kyle's clothes and suitcase were hanging in the closet, his toiletries were already next to the marble sink in the lavish bathroom, and the room felt full of his presence. I couldn't believe how much I missed him, even though it had been only one night.

First, I opened the gift bag, wanting to save the letter for last—I had a feeling it would be special. Inside was the perfect pair of earrings shining in a silk-lined box. Delicate and precious, they were diamonds and amethysts to match the colors and feel of the wedding theme.

I tore open the letter and began to read:

Happy wedding day, my soon-to-be wife!

I can't believe I will get to call you that for the rest of my life. I love you so much and cherish every moment we get to spend together. I couldn't imagine doing this crazy life without you by my side. Thank you for your love, support, and thoughtfulness daily. I'm so blessed God brought you into my life. I hope this day is everything you dreamed of and more. You deserve it. You are such an amazing person, thank you for everything that you do for me. I love that we have so much fun together, but also that when times are hard, I always have you in my corner.

You are my rock, my love, my wife.

I melted into the pure love I felt in that moment. In just a few hours, I was going to marry the man of my dreams—the man who loved that I am a challenge, who always held my hand, touched my leg under the table, and placed his hand in the small of my back while holding the door open for me. He was my partner in every sense of the word, the man who always made me feel like I was the most important person in his life. He was my teammate and my true other half. Kyle believed in my dreams, and he drove me toward my goals and supported me.

I could not believe this was real. In just a few hours, I would be married. I turned my head and saw my wedding gown hanging on the closet door. My breath caught in my throat at its beauty.

It was an off-the-shoulder mermaid dress, featuring a sweetheart neckline splashed with a variety of clear, sparkly jewels that wrapped around to the back. The back was exquisite—a fine mesh, encrusted with a pattern of jewels that looked as though my skin itself had been decorated. The dress ended in a dramatic train with a soft explosion of white feathers along the bottom. And there on the dresser next to that masterpiece was my bouquet: hundreds of rose petals meticulously crafted to create the illusion of one giant bloom nestled in a mist of white feathers.

From this vantage point, I watched the second act of our own Broadway show unfolding downstairs. The best wedding planning team in the business danced about below me in a flurry of hands as the stylists' makeup brushes whirled to the music of happy, laughing women sharing precious minutes and heartfelt joy on a momentous day. A chorus line of waitstaff continued to bring trays of food and drinks. The women who checked their makeup in the bright mirrors looked like beautiful starlets getting ready for showtime. I smiled to myself, enjoying the production.

Before long, I heard my mother's feet on the stairs, coming up to the bedroom to help me dress. She let herself in and came to me on the balcony. Taking my hands in hers, she looked into my eyes and said, "I hope someday you are as blessed as I am right now and can share this moment with your own daughter. You're the most beautiful and loving daughter, sister, niece, and friend to everyone you meet. I'm so proud of the woman you are and everything you have already accomplished. I know in my heart that today will be the day you've always dreamed about, and that you'll live your life with Kyle with the grace, determination, and strength with which you've always lived. I love you so very much."

We talked about the past and about the future as she helped me into the dress, slowly fastening each delicate clasp on my back. Just as she finished with the last one, I heard a gasp from the door. I turned my head and saw my father staring at the two of us.

"Hi, Pops," I said to my dad, using the name I've called him since I was a child. I smiled wide and saw his eyes fill with tears.

"Wow," he said, his voice cracking with emotion, "you look so beautiful." He came across and lovingly wrapped his arm around my mother's waist. Taking it all in, he smiled and said, "Nonnie would have loved to see this— your grandmother always said you would make the most beautiful bride." He cleared his throat and continued in a voice thick with emotion, "Even though you're getting married, you'll always be my little girl, and I will always, always be here for you no matter what you need or when you need it."

Pops then asked, "Are you ready? It's time to go to the church—unless you're having second thoughts, and then I'll help you run away." He winked, and I laughed, and the final curtain dropped on the pre-wedding matinee. The main event was about to start. I took his arm and exited the suite, stage left.

We left the hotel without jackets—a miracle of its own for Chicago in winter—and saw my chariot awaiting: a 1920s Rolls Royce Phantom in brilliant white. My father opened the back door for me, and we had a laugh as we tried to figure out how to get my dress—and all eight feet of its train—into the back seat. When we were seated inside at last, I looked like I was perched on a cloud of marshmallow fluff. Pops ran around the car and hopped in next to the driver, and soon we were off.

Sitting in that stunning car behind my father, I was reminded of that first fateful ride-along I had taken with Kyle when I was a college student in Indianapolis. While this was much slower, it felt right to be starting and ending our courtship with me riding in cars with the men who were the most important to me in the world.

A few short minutes later, we arrived at Holy Name Cathedral. It was a sight to behold, with giant bronze doors. The spire jutted into the sky, and on that day, it felt like a monument to the love that Kyle and I shared. I was so ready to marry him that, if I could have, I would have dashed from the car, skipped the ceremony altogether, and married him that second.

Susan, the wedding planner, ushered us through a side door out of view of the guests and suddenly it was happening. So much of what Kyle and I had been through ran through my mind. The first time I flew to visit him in Texas, our first kiss, the long nights I spent in my college apartment talking and studying as we got to know each other from a distance, moving to Charlotte, and every single step of the way standing strong beside each other. Soon, the organ's music began playing, and I saw the wedding party couple up before starting their slow walk down the aisle to the altar. When Wagner's *Bridal Chorus* began to play on the organ, I took Pop's hand. He looked me in the eyes, whispered that I was going to have the most beautiful life, kissed me on the cheek, and covered my face with my bridal veil.

I heard our wedding planner and her assistant count to three, and then in unison they swung the two giant doors open. When I walked through the church before, it had always been empty. I had marveled over the sweeping dark-chocolate ceiling over pointed stone arches. An intricate latticework of hardwood adorned the ceiling, and vibrant stained-glass windows let colorful, dancing light stream into the Gothic interior. But, on this day, I hardly noticed. Instead, I could only see the huge church full of people I loved standing on their feet to watch me walk down the aisle. I leaned into my father as we walked, the gauzy veil giving a sense of otherworldliness to everything I saw. Cameras flashed; new friends and old waved and blew kisses as we proceeded up the aisle to the sanctuary.

Where Kyle waited for me.

As soon as I saw him, everyone else disappeared. He looked so hand-some wearing a black tuxedo with a pink rosebud on his lapel, but it was the way he was looking at me that made my breath catch. I could *see* how much he loved me. With the back of his hand, my stoic soon-to-be husband wiped away brimming tears. In this giant church full of the people who meant the most to us, the two of us were alone.

When we arrived near the altar, Kyle descended the few stairs to the communion rail to shake my father's hand. They exchanged friendly words, Kyle promising to take care of me, and my father wishing him well, and then suddenly my father was lifting my veil. I blinked and the room came into sharp detail as my father kissed me on the cheek with a bittersweet swirl of sadness and pride and happiness in his tear-filled eyes and turned to take his seat.

I was all Kyle's, and he took my hand and helped me up the steps to the altar.

Ours was a traditional Catholic ceremony. We said our vows before God in this holy place, and we promised in the presence of the people we cared about the most to always love each other. I remember our priest's voice filling the church, echoing above in the high, arched ceilings. It felt holy, and sacred, and blessed in this most special of places.

The priest didn't need to tell Kyle twice that he could kiss the bride. He did, and the room exploded in applause and happy cheers.

I was Mrs. Kyle Busch. Hand in hand, we nearly skipped down the aisle as the organ played a bright and happy recessional. Our cheeks hurt from smiling so broadly as people leaned out into the aisle to kiss us, shake our hands, and congratulate us as we passed.

Now it was time to party.

Our wedding was traditional, but our reception was anything but. We didn't spend time on formalities or traditions. We wanted to have a true celebration—it was New Year's Eve, after all. Kyle and I danced with our friends and family, laughing and feeling fully alive. We wanted this part of the night to be fun, and it was. The room was full of love and energy, and when it came time for us to leave, nobody wanted the party to end. A smiling, excited crowd wrapped their arms around one another and chanted, "Hell no, we won't go!" as the lights came up and the band finished its last song.

As the curtain fell on the final act of the evening's show, Kyle and I exited the stage, man and wife.

7

DECIDING TO BECOME THREE

In the middle of the third NASCAR season after our wedding, we had a week off. Since Kyle and I were spending basically every weekend at the racetrack between Valentine's Day and Thanksgiving, these breaks were precious. We decided to spend it in sunny Cabo, Mexico. Cabo is a special place, where the beaches stretch horizon to horizon and the world's best margaritas can be found.

The salt air complemented our sweet drinks perfectly, and when I say the resort was stunning, I mean it. Cacti and other native plants were crafted into living art, connecting us to the foreign landscape while the warm sun quickly erased the stress of the racing season. We held hands as we approached our villa and laughed at the two fat iguanas perched outside our door.

"Looks like we've got some new pets," I joked.

The villa was magical. Enormous wooden doors were inlaid with exquisite stained-glass accents. I laughed out loud as Kyle scooped me into his arms and carried me over the threshold, where a larger-than-life window filled the room with golden sunshine. The dining table was adorned with fresh margaritas along with homemade chips and salsa. A pool divided the two wings of the house, and we could swim from one side of the house to the other.

Life was good.

We lost track of time as we spent days relaxing by the water, exploring Cabo, and eating some of the best meals I've ever had in local restaurants. We spent the nights making love and reconnecting. Gone were the schedules, responsibilities, and obligations of our normal lives. We talked a lot about our childhoods, thinking about our parents and the lives they'd built for us, and fantasized together about where our future would take us.

One day as Kyle and I were sitting by the pool, I smiled at him as the sound of old races drifted from his phone—even when relaxing, he's a racer through and through. I left him to it and started scrolling through my social media—which was quickly filling with baby announcements, selfies of rounded pregnant bellies, and the most beautiful babies with the chubbiest cheeks.

They called to a deep, secret, and scared part of me. I had always wanted kids, but when I looked around at the quiet beauty around me, I reflected on the perfect life Kyle and I were living. We had almost everything we wanted—and for this girl from Indiana, we had more than I ever dreamed of having. Our free time was ours—we could fly to Cabo or just spend the days off at home watching Netflix together. We could go on hikes or stay up all night playing games and talking. We almost never fought—Kyle and I thought so much alike on so many important issues that there wasn't much to fight about.

What would a baby do to us?

I had visions of our pristine vacation melting away into a pile of dirty diapers, middle-of-the-night feedings, and the nonstop stickiness of spit-up on my shoulder. And what if Kyle and I disagreed over how to raise our kids? Would the magical friendship and powerful love we shared change when there was someone else in our family?

To be honest, part of me wanted to be selfish. I wanted to keep Kyle to myself and keep living the life we had. I mean, let's be real—our life was pretty easy in a lot of ways. I was aware of how blessed we were, and a part of me really wanted to hold on to this stage of our lives together a little bit longer. But I saw how happy my friends were. I remember seeing the look on the face of one of my girlfriends in a picture she posted just after giving birth. This tiny, wrinkly, terrified little creature sat naked against the bare skin of her chest, opening its eyes for the first time and peering into hers, buried in sweaty strands of hair and a face flushed from the effort of pushing.

She should have been exhausted beyond feeling, but the *bliss* on her face—it was angelic. It seemed holy even, as though she had become a vessel of faith and was looking into the divine. The images were so powerful that they seemed to reach out from the screen and touch a part of me in a profound way.

I wanted to feel that too, so badly. I wanted to know the warmth of that baby on my skin, and I wanted to be the first thing new eyes ever see. The new eyes of my child.

While throughout our time together Kyle and I had shared very casual conversations or jokes about being parents, I decided it was time to talk seriously with him about having a baby. Laying there in my bikini, I slid my phone over to him with the photo of my pregnant friend filling the screen.

"What do you think? Would you still want me to wear this if we were having a baby?"

He eyed me up and down, and I could feel his eyes all over me. "I'll always want you to wear that. As far as the baby? I'm open to it, sure. But we wouldn't be able to be here," as he gestured to the peace and beauty of our surroundings.

This started one of the best, most important discussions of our marriage. We wondered if it was a good time, and then realized there will never be a good time with the kind of life we have. We talked about whether we could make a child work in our fast-paced lives that took us on the road so many days out of the year. From multiple businesses to races, appearances, and everything else we juggled, would we be able to manage it all with a child too?

But we also imagined a future full of children's laughter. Kyle imagined having a son who loved racing as much as he did, who he could teach about cars and share his passion with in a way he had never been able to before. I pictured a perfect little daughter, wearing an outfit that matched mine as I taught her how to braid her hair, and later on being a best friend and confidante to a self-assured young woman learning to find her own way in the world.

The afternoon went on like this—not stressful or confrontational, but transforming. We were sitting at the top of a summit, with two paths down. Both led to beautiful valleys, but we could only choose one of them. As we shared our hopes and our fears, listing the pros and cons of starting a family, I felt the valley of motherhood calling me. I could see the way down the path, cluttered with toys, with shorter nights and longer days, but it looked beautiful to me. It called to me.

As our vacation stretched out, our tans darkened. We danced late into the nights and shared barefooted walks along the beach. The warm ocean water washed the fine sand from our feet, erasing our footsteps, making it look like we just appeared where we were on the pristine beach. We held hands, joined together at the edge of a continent with the Pacific Ocean out in front of us, full of unknown wonders and fears. It seemed fitting as we stood on the edge of our own private ocean, deciding whether or not to swim into parenthood's deep and uncertain waters.

When we woke up late in the morning of our last day in paradise, Kyle mentioned he had a surprise planned for dinner that evening. I am *terrible* with surprises and begged him to let me know, pestering for clues, but he was a vault, keeping his secrets to himself as he went to play a round of golf while I happily spent the afternoon by the pool.

As the shadows lengthened and afternoon stretched into evening, I stepped into our outdoor shower, where I was surrounded by bright, fragrant tropical plants. The warm water washed the salt from my hair. I wanted this exact moment to last forever, and at the same time I was excited for our future. Stepping out of the shower, I dried off with the thick, soft terrycloth towels the hotel provided and pulled on the most luxurious robe. As I sat at the vanity to blow-dry my hair, my phone sounded a sharp "ding" to let me know a text had arrived. It was my mother, letting me know a cousin of mine was pregnant with her second child. My cousin was only two years older than me, and while part of me felt I was far too young to have a child at twenty-six, I saw her as a strong and happy mother of two at almost the same age.

I turned off the hairdryer just as Kyle returned. He stepped up in front of me and bent to place a kiss on my forehead. "You're going to love the surprise I have for you tonight," he said as he turned on some music and started getting dressed. Watching him in the gilded mirror, I began to imagine what he would be like as a father. I smiled as I saw him trying to raise daredevils while I wrapped them in Bubble Wrap to protect them from harm. I could see him placing a Band-Aid over a skinned knee as he cheered our child back onto the bike she had just fallen off. In my mind's eye, I saw him give our daughter away at her wedding, trying to hide the tear he wiped out of the corner of his eye, and I imagined him teaching our son to drive at an age far lower than might be legal in any state. Every part of him as a father made sense to me.

Kyle finished dressing just as I finished curling my hair. He wrapped his arms around me from behind and kissed my neck. "Ready to join me for dinner?" As we walked down the path to the restaurant, we encountered a family we'd met during the trip. The father carried a young chestnut-haired girl in a dandelion-yellow dress. Her tired head was tucked into his shoulder, and my heart melted. Kyle knew, and I felt him squeeze my hand as we exchanged pleasantries with the parents.

Before we reached the restaurant, I felt Kyle pull me down a side path toward the beach. "But the restaurant's this way," I laughed, tugging him back. "Come with me," he said, and I followed down the path with the gentle sound of the waves masking our footfalls. Ahead of me, I saw the warm, yellow glow of candlelight glinting off silverware. A table for two was set on the beach, its crisp white linens tinted orange by the dancing torches lighting the table.

"Surprise," whispered Kyle as a waiter materialized seemingly out of thin air.

"Mr. and Mrs. Busch, may I seat you for your private dinner?" He presented us with two flutes of chilled champagne as he walked us down to the table. He pulled my chair out as Kyle waited for me to sit. I was awestruck by the romance and overwhelmed by the sights and sounds of the evening, but more than that, it was Kyle who took my breath away. He looked as handsome as I'd ever seen him in his white linen button-down shirt, his freshly shaved cheeks slightly pink from the sun, and his just-right hair gelled exactly the way I liked it.

As the expert staff brought drinks and food and melted away into the darkness of the night, Kyle and I again discussed our hopes for and fears of a future as parents. That night, we grew up. As we held hands across the table with the last of our plates whisked away into the night, I looked into his eyes and saw a father, and I knew he saw a mother in mine. It was time for us to take the first step down the path that led to becoming a family.

8

BABY ON THE BRAIN

Once we'd made the decision to have a baby, I was all baby all the time. I'm a Type-A personality and a planner, and there was no little thing I was willing to leave to chance. I remember a conversation I had with my friend Tara that was typical of many of the conversations I had during this time in my life.

"So, Kyle and I are going to have a baby," I gushed. We were at my favorite local brunch place, and I swirled a gently bubbling mimosa around in its glass as we spoke.

After the usual excitement, squealing, and hugging, we got down to the details.

"Have you started trying?" she asked, taking a sip of her spicy Bloody Mary, "because that's the fun part!"

"Oh no, not yet. I have a plan. I think kids' birthday parties are way more fun in the summer: there's swimming and water balloon fights, barbecues, and campouts; there are super-fun outdoor games, and longer days so birthdays seem more special. We're going to get pregnant this fall."

I could see her eyes widening, but I was just getting started. The waiter brought our meals. I dug in as I continued, "I mean, even summer desserts are better. Right? There's this Hawaiian Jell-O bowl with candy fish floating in it that my mom used to make for all my June birthday parties, and I want my daughter to have that too."

With a growing look of unease, Tara drained the rest of her cocktail and signaled for another. I kept right on going, "Then, we can announce around Christmas, which would just be magical. Our Christmas cards will feature Kyle and me kissing while holding an ultrasound picture. We'll have lights strung up in pine trees as snow gently falls behind us. Can't you see it? Or maybe in the spring, which is the *perfect* time to announce a new baby, right? Easter and new flowers and grass and baby animals everywhere? Our announcement can be totally cheesy and say something adorable like we are so *EGGcited* that our own little bunny is on the way. Do you think Kyle would wear bunny ears?" I think Tara might have been about to call for help.

"But I'm coming off the pill now because I've read that it takes time for it to get out of my system and I *have* to be ready by October. Also, summer baby clothes are the cutest. I saw the most adorable little pink ruffled bikini with glitter on it the other day that I just had to buy!" I practically shrieked in delight, imagining my adorable little butterball poolside with me.

Tara looked like she wanted to know who the crazy person sitting across the table from her was, and what she had done with her friend.

"Samantha," Tara said a little boozily, "your wedding planning was over the top. Your baby planning can't even *see* the top. You know it's not as easy as snapping your fingers and 'boom,' there's a baby, right?"

"Well, no, Tara, snapping fingers isn't usually how people do that," I quipped. "But look! You weren't even trying, and BOOM, you had a baby."

The fact that I was going to be pregnant in just a few months was all I could think about. If there was a book about how to get pregnant, I read it. I spent hours Googling cute maternity outfits for early spring, when I envisioned my bump really beginning to show. I read blogs and websites of new moms talking about their pregnancies and beyond, the best creams to avoid stretch marks, the benefits of having a birth photographer during delivery, and whether it was safe to co-sleep or not.

I had an ovulation tracker, a macro diet tracker, a heart rate tracker. I'd sit in the pit box as Kyle was racing and study up on month-by-month pregnancy symptoms and read medical journals on the best foods to eat for peak fertility. I'd get dressed and look in the mirror, imagining a big, round, swollen belly stretching the material I was wearing tight across it.

My favorite app showed how big the baby was each week by comparing it to a piece of fruit. It went through every single week, from blueberry to watermelon; and I could not wait to take pictures of my growing body, my growing *baby,* and share them with the world like the adorable bump updates pictures I obsessed about on Instagram.

And then there were the baby names. I wanted names that were cool, different, and exciting—but not *too* different. I read over their meanings, listened to songs and read books for inspiration, and packed so many Pinterest boards with so many baby products, nursery ideas, quotes, and dreams for what was to come.

When I was out shopping, I'd buy cute little boy and girl outfits and leave the tags on, planning to return the ones we wouldn't be using when we found out if we were having a boy or a girl. And for when we did find out the gender, I spent hours watching YouTube videos for the coolest gender reveal party ideas so we could share the moment with family and friends.

While I have always paid attention to my diet and exercise, I took my fitness to a whole new level. I read every article on pregnancy nutrition I could find. New supplements like CoQ10, fish oil, and turmeric filled my medicine cabinet, and I swapped out my daily vitamins for whole food–based prenatal vitamins. I added extra protein and healthy fats to my diet and went out and bought a big juicer. Soon, I was drinking vibrant green baby-making smoothies every day. If Dr. Oz said to eat it, it went into my rotation. Daily yoga added a level of Zen to my day, keeping me limber and relaxed. I wanted my body to be the absolute best temple it could be for my child to grow.

The only thing left to do was to put a bun in the oven.

I wanted the first time Kyle and I tried to get pregnant to be special. I mean, it *was* special—this was the first step to the next phase of our life together. It felt momentous. I wanted it to be memorable. To set the mood, I made one of Kyle's favorite meals: spaghetti with my homemade sauce. It was my Nonnie's recipe she'd brought from Italy, and as I chopped garlic and fresh basil, I thought that since she had six kids, this sauce was going to be a good-luck charm.

I stirred in salt and seasonings and Nonnie's secret ingredients and imagined what this kitchen would look like in a year. Baby locks would keep the cabinets closed, and a high chair would sit safely away from the stove so our baby could be with me while I cooked. Colorful toys would litter the counter, and bottles and pacifiers and all the other accoutrements of babyhood would be everywhere. It was a happy daydream as I slowly stirred the sauce.

With the pot bubbling away and the richly seasoned scent of the sauce filling the house, I got ready for Kyle. First, I needed to select just the right lingerie for the occasion. Black seemed too dark. Red felt forced—I wanted to feel naturally sexy. Pink was too cute. Finally, I selected a sheer, white lace bodysuit. White seemed appropriate, pure even. To wear over it, I picked a low-cut top with just enough lace to be seen when I bent over. I was planning on being seen.

I tugged up a pair of skinny jeans and realized that hopefully soon my jeans would be the only skinny thing about me. I needed something else, though, a special touch that connected us to the love we started our family with and were going to grow.

And then I knew. I opened my jewelry box and selected the earrings

Kyle gave to me before our wedding. They were exactly the right thing, a symbol of all we are and all we are trying to become.

As I made my way back to the kitchen to carefully check the sauce, I realized that these might be the last few hours of my life when I was not a *mother*. My heart swelled, and excitement built in my belly. Then I heard Kyle arrive home.

Quickly, I lit the candles on the table, dimmed the lights in the dining room, and started playing John Mayer through the speakers. Kyle walked in, took in the room, then looked at me and cracked the biggest smile. It's not every day he comes home to candles, wine, and me in full makeup and heels. He knows me well. "And what are we doing tonight?" he asked as he took me in his arms. "Are we 'officially' trying?"

"I stopped taking the pill yesterday."

We both knew that this could take time, that one day off the pill was not an instant invitation to pregnancy. But it felt powerful in that moment, like the first time you say, "I love you," to someone you want to spend your life with. He sat at the table, ready to start with the special meal I prepared for him. I crossed the room, sat in his lap, and kissed him deeply.

Our dinner ended up being late and very cold, and we were perfectly fine with that.

9

PRACTICE DOESN'T MAKE PERFECT

I n the beginning, there was sex.

A whole lot of sex. It was exciting—a whirlwind of spontaneous lovemaking, fun lingerie, and lingering sappy moments. It felt like the perfect combination of wild and loving, almost like a second honeymoon. We were reinvigorated with the possibility of becoming parents, and each caress felt like a giddy act of creation.

After we made love, I would lie in bed (or on the kitchen table, or the floor, or wherever we happened to finish) wondering if this was the time that would lead to a baby. I tried to imagine what conception would feel like—would I know when it happened? Would I feel a cramp or a tickle or an innate sense of motherhood? Or would I just be surprised one day when my period didn't come?

Speaking of periods, mine was all over the place. Sometimes they were two weeks apart, sometimes five. Sometimes I would feel it coming, and sometimes it would just start on its own. At first, I didn't worry too much about it—after coming off the pill, this could happen, and I'd been on the pill for a long time. I was in a bubble of happiness, especially connected to Kyle, and loving every minute.

Of course, bubbles always pop. Every new period, and the few times I took and failed a pregnancy test, seemed to deflate that bubble and make it harder to blow up again. So, I decided to take matters into my own hands. I knew I had a clean bill of health from my OB-GYN, and they told me they wouldn't even begin to be concerned about our not conceiving until we had been trying for at least a year. I asked them that question *a lot*, and they told me the same thing every time.

But Dr. Google was always there for me, and I spent day after day looking for tips because I was starting to get impatient. The most common suggestion was to start tracking my ovulation. This seemed smart for several reasons, most important, because my periods were still coming and going like an indoor-outdoor cat.

It turns out the internet had many suggestions about how to track your ovulation. Some of them were not my favorite. For example, it told me to check my cervical mucus. Sounded interesting, so I clicked away and immediately my jaw hit the floor. How do you check your cervical mucus, you ask? Well, apparently, you insert your finger deep into your vagina, pull out some secretions, and rub them across your fingers to see if they were the consistency of egg whites. If so? It's time to make a baby. Gross. Nope. No, that was not high on my to-do list, so I quickly clicked the back button and moved on.

The next result was more up my alley—drive on down to the local drugstore and buy an ovulation testing kit! I wondered why that didn't come up before I tried to make mucus meringue as I hopped into the car happy to make a purchase. When I got home, I tore the kit open and learned that I had to pee on a stick. Well, *that* I could handle. On the days I was ovulating or close to it, the stick was supposed to show a happy face. Cute!

I wanted to keep things interesting, so along with the kit I bought some organic lube (no chemicals were getting near *my* baby's DNA!) and a vibrating toy and waited for that smiley face to appear. As luck would have it, it happened the very next morning. I showed Kyle the smiley face and told him it was time to have sex, to which he showed me his own smiley face.

Just a few days later, I got my period. I was crushed, I mean really devastated. I didn't understand how I was just ovulating and now I have my period. I called my OB-GYN—by this point I had them on speed dial—and was a little reassured when they told me that some women just take a little longer to get back to regular and to keep trying.

Month after month, we tried and we tried. With every period and every negative test, I became more and more obsessive. Distraught, I dove down the deep, dark hole of the internet and tried to find anything at all I was missing in my healthy baby-focused lifestyle. Even if it didn't make sense to me, I added it to my daily routine. One nurse at my OB-GYN office told me to drink more water, and despite rolling my eyes, I was trying everything so I drank gallons of the stuff. This helped, but only because I was peeing on so many sticks. But I didn't get it—were my eggs dehydrated? Another said to not drink liquor. Hadn't they ever heard of tequila leading to babies? The weirdest suggestion was "eat a pineapple core." I couldn't even figure out how to eat that, so I passed. Relax more, people said. I'm go-go-go all the time, but I tried.

And then we were back to the cervical mucus. This time, I tried it. Guess what? Still gross. Still didn't work.

I spent as much time digging into what might be up with Kyle's little swimmers as I did looking into my own body. One particular tidbit jumped out at me: turns out, sperm like cool environments. This is why it's boxers over briefs if you're trying to get pregnant. It also means guys need to keep out of the sauna, hot baths, and tight bathing suits (and let's face it—guys should just stay out of tight bathing suits regardless).

Well, Kyle spends a *lot* of time inside a hot racecar. If it's 90 degrees outside, it's 130 degrees in the car. Kyle's job was baking my baby batter! This would not do. So, I broached the subject with him, armed with medical evidence.

"What? Do you want me to put ice on my balls?" he asked.

"YES!" I shouted. "Exactly! Thank you, thank you!" I covered him with kisses.

He looked much less happy than I was. "Well," he groaned, "the guys already give me bags of ice to put in my suit to keep me cool, I guess I could shove one of them down a little lower." One of the things I love about him is that even when I was being crazy, he was supportive.

That weekend at the race, I watched his crew hand him an ice pack and laughed out loud in the pit box. It was our little secret, but his chilly little sperm had to be happier.

Now, throughout all this I was continuing to track my ovulation on those pee sticks.

They all said the same thing: I was ovulating. So why wasn't I pregnant? And then it hit me like a meteor in my obsessive brain: If we had sex every single day, we couldn't *possibly* miss my ovulation window. There would always be swimmers in the sea! I told Kyle my plan, and I swear to God he gave me a high five. This was something he could get behind. And in front of, and on top of.

And at first, we did. Different positions. Different parts of the house. Different times of day. Quickies and not-so-quickies. It wasn't always easy to make it work given our crazy schedules, but I was on a mission: get those sperm to the egg. As the mission wore on, though, it started to be less fun and became more like a chore. I think Kyle developed a limp. He began to appreciate the ice on his boys.

There was so much added pressure that sex stopped being any fun at all. It was *work*. We didn't want to set the wrong tone or put a strain on our relationship, but stress crept in regardless. Sex became mechanical. We needed to be precise when it came to re-creating the exact positions the internet said would facilitate procreation.

I started bringing the iPad to bed to show Kyle what I wanted him to do with the help of diagrams.

"No, honey. See how it says to hold my leg at a 50 degree angle? You're at about 35." I held up the screen so he could see just how bad his geometry skills were—not exactly dirty talk.

By day twenty-three, we just couldn't do it anymore.

"Babe," Kyle said to me, "I think I'm just shooting air at this point. There's nothing left down there. Pass the ice, please."

I was sad, angry, relieved, and confused. I was a mess. I just didn't understand how this could not be happening. It felt like I had drained Kyle dry of sperm. I had achieved the impossible in driving a man to the point where he didn't want to have sex anymore. And still nothing. We were at our wits' end.

But then something that seemed miraculous happened: My period didn't come. I was still irregular by medical standards, but it had been months since I had gone this long between periods, and I knew as sure as I knew my name that I was pregnant. I could *feel* it; it was in my marrow and in my womb. And so, I rummaged through the cabinet for my supply of pregnancy tests for the last time (I knew it) and called Kyle to the bathroom with me. I didn't mean to tell him this way, but I was never good at keeping secrets.

He stood there while I peed, awkward and excited as you only can be when someone is peeing next to you to find out if you are going to be a father. Bright light shone in our window, reminding me of the sunlight streaming into our wedding. I rested the dripping stick on the side of the sink to wait two minutes, two years, to find out.

We talked about how life was going to be different, about how we had to start getting the nursery ready, about far too many things for two minutes. And then the timer went off.

I leapt to the sink and grabbed the stick.

One. Blue. Line.

Not pregnant.

I collapsed to the floor, disbelieving, defeated, sobs shaking my frame. Kyle, stoic and strong as always, held me as I cried. We should be pregnant. We were ready to be parents, to have a child to love and nurture, to have someone call us Mommy and Daddy. I *knew* we were pregnant, but we weren't. The once-cheery sunshine now seemed harsh, a stark contrast to the pain and darkness inside me. I don't know how long we lay there—until my eyes were red and swollen and all the tears had found their way onto the bathroom floor. Kyle helped me to my feet. My not-mother feet. For the first time, we felt utterly defeated.

We didn't know the worst was still to come.

10

TRYING TIMES

I became a sex Nazi. We were now ten months into trying to have a baby, and with each failed test I became more and more despondent. Sex became a chore, something Kyle and I both dreaded because it wasn't fun; it wasn't done as an act of love or pleasure or connectedness anymore. It was all about procreation, all the time. There was no lovemaking; this was sex with a different purpose, and it was driving Kyle and me apart.

After sex, we used to lie in each other's arms, laughing or talking or just being together. Now, as soon as we finished, I would throw my legs in the air and he'd shove pillows under my butt because I had read that this can help in conception. He would go and do his thing, and I'd stay there crying, pleading with God to let this be the time I got pregnant. I was ashamed. To me, being a woman meant being able to have babies. My body was created to hold and grow a life inside it, and mine was empty, seemingly incapable of doing its job. I felt like a failure.

As my frustrations and pain mounted, I took them out on Kyle. He was the only person who knew the full extent of what was happening, so he bore the brunt of my anguish. When I saw pregnant friends on social media, or even a commercial for diapers, my mood could turn on a dime. More than that, I found it harder to be around people, as I was always fearful of inevitably being asked when Kyle and I would have kids.

As all this was happening, one of my best friends was pregnant. She and I had talked a little bit about the fact that Kyle and I were trying, but I never confided in her about the extent of the difficulties we were having and how my every waking moment was consumed with the idea of getting pregnant. And that's how it came to be that I volunteered to throw her baby shower.

By this point, I had mastered the art of being outwardly okay in public only to lose it completely when I was finally able to take off the mask. So, I planned the way I know how to. I chose the most perfect cupcakes with icing in shades of pink, stuffed bag after bag of party favors, and made fun pregnancy-themed games, always showing the world my perfectly composed and happy face.

The morning of the shower, I carefully strung decorations around the room with other friends, talking about how happy we were for our friend, and fantasizing about how adorable her baby would be. One friend, a new mother herself, wistfully mentioned the smell of a new baby in your arms, and suddenly my arms felt emptier than they have ever been. Still, I wore the mask, laughing when I needed to, wincing at the struggles of mother-hood when appropriate, and dying inside every minute of it.

Soon, the guests started arriving, and pregnant belly after pregnant belly turned up at my doorstep. It was a NASCAR baby boom. As the afternoon wore on, women asked when I would be having a shower of my own. I wanted to scream, but inevitably I found myself answering those questions with a grin plastered to my face.

"Someday," I'd say.

"When the time is right."

"Oh, you know, we'll get there."

I lied through my teeth to my friends and spent the day trying not to break down. Soon, I was sitting next to the mother-to-be, carefully recording every gift, watching outfits I had browsed for *my* baby gifted to someone else. As quickly as the gifts were opened, I busied myself in the kitchen, in the bathroom, anywhere where I might not have to endure any baby talk.

The unfairness of it nearly overwhelmed me. I hated feeling this jealous of the women I loved in my life. I wanted so badly to be completely happy for them, but I couldn't manage it. When the last guest finally left, I was emotionally exhausted, refusing to speak to anyone—even Kyle.

The worst betrayals were when my body gave me false hope. One warm morning as I was working around the house, I started getting intense cramping, unlike any I had ever had. I'd read that this could be a sign of ovulation, so I sent Kyle a text.

"Come home please, I'm ovulating."

Ten minutes passed, and he didn't respond, so I sent another text. "Urgent—come home right away."

Now, Kyle was in a meeting, and I knew he was in a meeting, but I could not help myself. I was so invested in this process, and we had endured so much, that it blew my mind he wouldn't stop whatever he was doing to come home and do this with me. What if we missed our one chance? Twice more, in shorter and shorter intervals, I sent texts trying to get his attention, but of course I didn't hear back—he was working. I just couldn't take it. Finally, I texted again: "DO YOU NEED A FUCKING INVITATION TO MY VAGINA? WHERE THE HELL ARE YOU??!!!!"

If that's not a turn-on, I don't know what is.

A couple of hours later, Kyle did return home, and it went about as you'd expect. We had a huge fight because while I was waiting, my cramping stopped. I was sure we had missed the window, and I blamed him. We still ended up having sex, but it was almost hate-sex. There was no tenderness, no affection, no pleasure. It was like assembling IKEA furniture: "Repeatedly insert Tab A into Slot B."

He stormed out when we were finished, and I got myself into a yoga headstand in the corner because I had read that *this* was something that could help. Upside down, legs in a corner, I seethed. If I got pregnant this time, this was going to be an *angry* baby, I just knew it.

We went to bed that night still not speaking, backs facing each other, angry. This was not who we were, but it was who we had become.

When I woke up, I had my period—the true source of the cramps that sparked my fight with Kyle the day before. I sat on the toilet and cried my heart out.

Sadness filled me on the inside, but on the outside I plastered a mask on, fake smiles and bright eyes that never fully concealed what was happening behind them. I engaged in the pleasant chit chat and forced myself to have normal social interactions. I was hurt and embarrassed and desperately sad. Despite being surrounded by people, I had never felt more alone in my life. I was disappearing—the outgoing, sparkly, and bubbly woman I had always been was sinking beneath a tide of despair. There were no life preservers. There was only the idea of a baby, drifting away on the horizon as I was consumed by my own anguish.

I knew I had a wonderful support system full of people who loved me and who deeply cared, but I didn't think anyone could understand the depth of the pain I was feeling. I didn't think I could find the words to explain what I was feeling and was embarrassed when I tried.

I was ready to pull my hair out.

Except I didn't need to because it started falling out on its own. What used to be a normal lock of hair that I would pull out of a shower drain became huge hunks that would clump together and wave in the water like seaweed as they flowed down the drain. I began to notice hard white bumps on my chest, like an undesired cobblestone road across my body that I could do nothing to contain. My jawline—my dad always said it was like a classic movie star's—sprouted angry red acne. And faster than I could pluck them, wiry hairs sprouted from my nipples. When my eyelashes started falling out, they were quickly replaced by coarse hair on my upper lip. I called my OB-GYN again and was again given a perfunctory statement about hormones being tricky and that this was nothing to worry about. I tried to stay as positive as I could but was not feeling myself either emotionally or physically.

It was as though the less desirable I felt, the less desirable I looked. When Kyle and I made love, I insisted that every light in the room be turned off and the shades drawn. I couldn't stand for him to see me. If he tried to caress my face, I'd turn away, not wanting him to feel the breakouts I was having—afraid that in the middle of all this he would stop being attracted to me. We still tried, both in our relationship and in our sex life, but it remained tense, sad, and so uncomfortable for both of us.

And then came the worst, final betrayal. I started bleeding heavily, more than I had ever bled. Great, rolling cramps wracked my abdomen. I was sure I was miscarrying—that somehow, I had finally conceived, but my body decided that I was unworthy of a baby. It was the final straw, the last thing I could take.

I left a frantic voicemail for my OB-GYN. Something was terribly wrong, I said. I got a call from her covering physician, who asked me to come into the office the next morning. All through that night, I tossed and turned, looking at the clock and finding it immobile. Dawn was hours away, it was days away, it was never going to come. When I couldn't wait at home any longer, I drove to the office, arriving half an hour before they opened. In the car, I bobbed one knee up and down with nervous energy as I listened to the morning's news without really hearing it.

When a staff member turned up to unlock the door to the office, I was out of the car in a shot and followed her into the office. I so desperately needed help, but I was afraid of what I was going to learn. It didn't help that I didn't have the relationship I wanted with my nurse practitioner.

Earlier visits left me feeling unheard and that my concerns were not taken seriously. But still, I couldn't do this anymore. I couldn't risk my body, which had already suffered so much, or my marriage, which was suffering even more, and I needed to find out what was happening to me. I fiddled with the light-blue cotton tie of the worn gown I was wrapped in. With each move, the paper on the table crinkled, crumpling the way I felt I was crumpling under the weight of my inability to get pregnant.

I went through the last year of everything I had experienced. I found myself unable to meet her eyes but gave her the most information I was able to summon. Without giving me much information or reassurance, she ordered the works: a full complement of blood labs, a physical exam, and an ultrasound. It was telling how emotionally and physically spent I was when the lab tech came in with her tray of needles and tubes and I barely even flinched. I'm the biggest baby around shots and needles, sometimes coming close to passing out—not that day.

With the first stick ("quick pinch," she said, although I've never been pinched and had it feel in any way like a needle), nothing happened. She moved the needle around under my skin, but the tube remained empty. My body was screwing me again. She moved to the other arm, and this time dark blood began to fill the tube, slow and red. When finished, she repeated the process twice more before asking me to hold a cotton ball over the tiny hole in my elbow.

The physical exam was thorough yet distant. I lay as still as I could on the frigid table while her gloved hands pressed down into my abdomen. I imagined her sterile hands pressing down into an empty cavern, nothing but space and darkness. She looked at the hair around my nipples and the acne on my face, walked her gloved fingers across the cobblestone road of white bumps on my chest. She finished her exam, but her face didn't reveal what she was thinking.

Then it was time for the ultrasound. I moved to another room, where it was very dark—an amber glow from the keyboard the only illumination.

The technician asked me to hop up on the table and get ready, and said she'd be right back. I reclined on the short vinyl surface, knees hanging down over the edge and the paper rustling beneath me. I rolled the gown up under my breasts, exposing my belly and covering my lower half with a paper sheet that had been left for me. I looked down at my belly, and tears sprang unbidden from my eyes. I quickly wiped them away when the ultrasound tech knocked on the door.

She saw me, belly ready for her probes, and said, "Oh, no. That's not how we do *these* ultrasounds." She helped me roll the gown back down while protecting my modesty and glanced over to the probe she would be using. It was long and straight like a pale wand wrapped in something reminiscent of a large plastic condom. I immediately understood what was happening with this and figured it would be about as loving and pleasurable as my sex life had been lately.

"Are you ready?" she asked, as I stared glassy-eyed at the probe.

I murmured my assent as she began the exam, first lubricating the probe and then as gently as she could inserting it into my body. I tensed, and watched the screen come to life in an unreadable pattern of grays and silvers and blacks. To me, everything looked like cancer, courtesy of Dr. Google. The tears came back, coursing down my cheeks as I tried to remain silent. This was not how it was supposed to be. This should have been Kyle and me, looking for toes and fingers and a perfect little chin. This was supposed to be the beginning of our journey, taken together.

It felt like an ending.

And just like that, it was over. She took out the probe, powered down the machine, and turned on the lights, shockingly bright in the too-small room.

"Am I okay?" I asked, pleading for reassurance.

"The doctor will read your scans and let you know what she sees," she responded, not unkindly, but with no room for argument.

Once I was alone, I took off the gown and tossed it angrily into the blue-bagged bin in the corner marked "Dirty Linen." On the way out, I made an appointment for two mornings later when I would learn the results.

That night and the next saw an uneasy truce at home, sexless and tense, but full of concern and underlying love. The morning we went back to the doctor, Kyle held me in bed for a few minutes before we got up, whispering that everything was going to be okay—we would find what was wrong and fix it—and reassuring me that he loved me and would be here. It was a tiny thaw in the icy life I was living, and I needed those words that morning.

We arrived at the appointment together and were quickly ushered into an exam room. The nurse practitioner came in shortly thereafter, flipping papers on a clear plastic clipboard. They seemed to be whispering, as though they were gossiping about the news they carried.

"We have your test results," she said. "Your progesterone levels are very low, and your testosterone level is high." She sounded like she was reading the stock reports from the back pages of the *Wall Street Journal* for all the passion she put into it. "Additionally," she continued, "the ultrasound revealed cystic ovaries. All of this coupled with your history of abnormal menstrual cycles means you have polycystic ovarian syndrome, or PCOS for short."

When I heard the word *syndrome,* I instantly had a panic attack and knew for sure I was dying. I burst into tears as she handed me a tissue.

"Why are you crying?" she asked gently, the first bit of tenderness seeping into her voice.

"Because I have a *syndrome,*" I said. "Is it life-threatening? Are cysts like cancer? Will I need surgery? Is this why we aren't pregnant?" Questions tumbled out of my mouth like water over a fall, one after the other with no room for breathing. Kyle put the brakes on and asked her for clarification, suggesting I take some deep breaths while she explained.

Clinically, she went into detail about what was wrong with my hormones and ovaries. She called up my ultrasound images on the computer. She pointed to my ovary on the screen. An almond-shaped area of lighter gray amid a sea of dark, covered with a multitude of tiny black specks.

"Do you see those dots?" she asked, pointing to one of the specks.

"Those are immature follicles, what we call cysts in your case. In normally functioning ovaries, a follicle matures and releases a mature egg. In your case, development of the follicle stops before the egg is mature, and you have many of them—hence the word *poly*—immature follicles with no mature eggs." She went on to explain that while the word *cyst* is alarming for many women, and some women do have ovarian cysts, in my case she reiterated they were just immature follicles. Isn't medical language fun?

She told me that PCOS has different effects on different women—some have irregular or no periods (check), or some lose their hair (check), or get acne (check) or hair on their face or other areas of their body (well, I had some whiskers), or gain weight (three out of four, I guess) due to their hormonal imbalances. The level of severity varies from person to person.

"So, what does it mean to have PCOS?" I understood the things she was telling me, but I wasn't sure I was grasping the big picture.

"Well," she answered, "it means that you have at least two of the following: irregular periods, problems with your ovaries like the immature follicles you have, and higher testosterone. You've got all three."

"And because your hormones are always out of whack," my doctor continued, "those ovulation kits you've been using are never going to work." The damned smiley faces had let me down. Dr. Google had let me down. My body had let me down.

I felt like so much time had been wasted and so much damage had been done to my relationship with Kyle. In my mind, I was to blame. All of this was because my body wasn't functioning properly. If I had just spoken up sooner and with more gusto, or opened up to others, or researched more, none of this would have been happening. My mind was overfull, chasing down rabbit hole after rabbit hole where only questions dwelled.

"Can I get pregnant?" I asked.

"I don't know," she answered.

She recommended I start a medication called Clomid. She explained it was a drug that tricked my body into thinking it had the appropriate levels of estrogen, which can stimulate follicle development and egg release. It was the first time I would hear the name Clomid, but definitely not the last. This was the start of a whole new chapter in our lives.

11

THE CLOMID CRAZIES

Every dose of Clomid should come with a giant neon warning sign: CAUTION: EXTREME EMOTIONS AHEAD. My family is Italian, and we are people with big emotions by nature. Add a daily dose of Clomid to the emotional roller coaster of the entire infertility process, and I was primed to blow. At times, I found myself feeling pent-up rage and fidgeting uncontrollably like a horde of angry fire ants inside me wanted to come out while, at other times, I felt perfectly normal—only to burst into tears over seemingly innocent events. During this ordeal I threatened to leave Kyle for the first and only time—over the movie *Titanic*. Really.

The day started in a fairly routine fashion. We were at the racetrack, and I spent the day working on small projects in the motorhome while Kyle handled his media obligations before the race. As the morning dwindled and shadows shrank under the noon sun, it was time for me to start what had turned into a monumental task: getting ready to appear in public.

I knew it was in vain, but I desperately wanted to hide from the world everything that was happening to me both internally and externally. Since I didn't have a team of stylists and makeup artists and psychologists to follow me around, even though I felt like I desperately needed them all, it was on me to make myself presentable. First, I slathered on skin serums to keep my raging acne at bay, then applied the concealers and foundations to hide the ever-present redness and inflammation in my skin. Since my hair was still falling out in great clumps, I clipped in long, curling hair extensions and teased and wrestled them into a semblance of a hairstyle. By the time I was done with all of my primping, those noonday shadows had lengthened and then disappeared altogether behind a front of heavy gray clouds.

Despite the threatening skies, the race got off as planned, but it wasn't long before the deluge started. We all started scurrying around like field mice below a kettle of hawks, desperate to find cover. I made it back to the bus, dripping and exhausted. One of my clip-on extensions hit the floor with a wet plop, the perfect metaphor for how I felt.

Before long, Kyle made it back to the motorhome. He found me flipping channels on the TV, where I settled on *Titanic,* which had just started. "It's going to be a while," he told me, "if we even get to start again today." I patted the cushion next to me. He looked at the TV warily and back to me.

"Sit. Down." I wasn't asking. With a sigh, he sank into the couch, and I lovingly snuggled into him. We watched Kate and Leo fall in love.

Two hours later, I was sobbing. Really ugly crying, with mascara running down my face and hiccups between sobs. I could *feel* the love that Leonardo DiCaprio's Jack had for Kate Winslet's Rose when (spoiler alert) he got her onto a door and sacrificed himself to the sea so that she could live. The courage and the nobility and the romance of it all moved me to my very core.

I turned my makeup-streaked, red-nosed, love-addled face toward Kyle, ready to see the true love on the screen reflected in his eyes, only to find him watching impassively with dry eyes and a vaguely bored look on his face. He was leaning all the way back on our deep couch, eyelids heavy in the dark room, and I was sure if I wasn't crying so loudly, he'd be snoring in a minute or two.

I could not believe it.

"What?" he asked, sensing my building fury.

"Can't you feel *anything*?" My arms started gesturing, big sweeps dangerously close to punches from across the couch.

"Sam, they're not real people. The boat sinks. We knew a lot of them were going to die. It's history, everybody knows it!"

Someone was going to die all right.

I lost it. I angrily jumped off the soft cushions as my rage burst out.

"I can't believe you! How can you be so callous? I can't have a baby with a man who can't feel love. True love. Are you telling me you wouldn't have let me have the door? I can't believe I married you. Do you even really love me? Actually, let me rephrase—do you really even know what love is? I don't think so. I'm done! I can't even speak to you anymore, let alone be in the same room as someone who clearly doesn't have any feelings!" I panted furiously and looked at him expectantly, daring him with my eyes to say anything.

Kyle blinked at me from the couch, trying desperately to contain a laugh that was working its way out of his mouth as I stormed out of the room, slamming doors behind me in an all-out rage.

I realized my mistake as soon as I stepped out of the motorhome and the pouring rain soaked through my formerly warm and dry pajamas. I stormed back in and shot knives out of my eyes at Kyle, who was still sitting bemused on the couch, and stalked off to the bedroom where I crumpled onto the soft duvet in a flood of tears. Eventually, I dozed off without knowing what I was really even crying about anymore.

Luckily, I came back to my senses overnight before I lost my marriage over the top date movie of 1996.

My flair for drama induced by this drug wasn't just reserved for Kyle. I had finally let my mom and a few close friends know what was going on in a cursory way. We hadn't yet had the full, therapeutic heart-to-hearts I so desperately needed because I wasn't ready to face it, but it was a start.

My mother suggested a girls' lunch out at Panera Bread where I ordered my go-to: a Thai chopped salad on spinach, add avocado, dressing on the side. We chatted away after placing our order, and I reveled in the fact that today I was finally feeling like my old self. After five months on Clomid, maybe my hormones were starting to adjust. Maybe this was finally the light at the end of the tunnel, and our time would soon be coming.

The pager I was given to let me know when our food was ready started buzzing and flashing crazily in my hand, so we made our way to the counter to claim our lunch. I glanced at my salad and found it was made not on spinach like I asked for but on romaine lettuce. Instantly, the rage I had not felt all day erupted out of me like a volcano. Hot, lava-like tears poured down my cheeks, and I shouted in the middle of the restaurant that the entire world was conspiring against me having a baby.

"What in the world are you talking about?" my mother asked under her breath, concern and dismay lining her face.

"The lettuce, Mom! Don't you understand I need to eat spinach for its iron, which will help me have a baby? I read it online—romaine doesn't have iron! I'm never going to get pregnant," I wailed in the middle of the restaurant, sniffling a running nose.

Having lost her appetite for some reason, my mom apologized profusely to the others in the restaurant and hustled me outside, muttering something about "her medicine." When we got home, we decided it was time to go back to the doctor before somebody got hurt.

Then I made what turned out to be one of the best phone calls of my life, although I didn't yet know it. At a visit the following week, my OB-GYN told me it was time to seek the help of a fertility clinic to figure out what was going on and gave me some names crisply printed on a sheet of paper.

It flapped around in my hand as I stepped out of that office for the last time, but I held on to it for dear life. I didn't know it then, but it turns out Romaine lettuce really can help you get pregnant.

12

REACHING OUT

Making the first call to REACH brought an unexpected mix of emotions. On one hand, we were finally *doing* something. It felt like we were taking back a little bit of control over a situation that had been driving our lives so far out of control they were hardly recognizable anymore. On the other hand, it was a surreal experience that felt like a surrender. All around us, couples were having babies naturally, with little to no effort—and even by accident—that it felt like the natural order was turned on its head.

I guess, when I look closely at it, *doubt* was the core of this feeling. I doubted myself as a woman. I doubted the just nature of creation. I even doubted my marriage. What if I couldn't get pregnant, even after we undergo fertility treatments? Would Kyle still want to be with me even if I could never carry his child? I was willing to go any route possible to have a child, but what if he wasn't? Would I ever be genuinely happy in life if I was never called Mommy? In the days that followed, this doubt was a constant presence, gnawing away at me in the dark, quiet hours of the night as Kyle snored gently beside me. I desperately wanted all these questions to be answered by a pregnancy, but I was also terrified of what the answers would be if I did not get pregnant.

I was also angry. I was angry at all the time we had wasted, all the unnecessary crushed hopes and broken hearts and the preventable stress. My OB-GYN had been insistent that we try for an entire year before undergoing any testing or treatment, which I now know is not the best practice recommended by fertility specialists. They suggest that since healthy couples generally get pregnant in the first six months of trying, earlier testing is better than waiting.

So, it was with some apprehension mixed with excitement and determination that Kyle and I entered the REACH clinic for the first time. Every seat in the room was filled with other couples radiating similar emotions: fear, uncertainty, excitement, guilt, sadness. The air felt thick with it, and the experience was disconcerting. Shortly after being welcomed warmly, we were introduced to Nurse Mary, a woman who almost seemed to glow with motherly demeanor and lovely brunette hair. She exuded calm, and I was instantly at ease. She explained a little bit about what was going to happen that day, which would include some blood tests and a meeting with Dr. Richard Wing, a highly regarded fertility specialist who'd founded the REACH clinic. She asked us if we had any questions before we started, and then guided us down the hall to Dr. Wing's spacious office.

Dr. Wing stood and stepped from behind his desk to shake our hands. Where Mary filled the area around her with warmth, Dr. Wing projected complete competence. It was easy to trust him right off the bat, and his professional, matter-of-fact demeanor complemented Mary's engaging personality perfectly. After the initial pleasantries, he pulled out a thin manila folder containing the medical records and test results my OB-GYN's office sent him. He read for a moment, turned the page, and made some small "hmm" sounds after he finished reading. Looking at Kyle, he asked, "Do you have your records with you?"

Confused, we looked at one another. "No, the problem is with me. It's my PCOS, not with Kyle." I wondered if I had misread Dr. Wing's competence—we'd spent months and months dealing with *my* problems. He had all the evidence right there in front of him in that folder. Did he really not know that already? It was a little infuriating. We had never hung such high hopes on anyone before, and this was not the best start.

"That's correct," he said, "but it might not be the whole story. We need to have Kyle's sperm tested too. It's possible that the Clomid might not have been the best treatment, depending on what Kyle's tests look like." My jaw dropped. *The Clomid might have been the wrong treatment?!* I thought back over all the crazy emotional days, the sudden anger and deep sadness that appeared out of nowhere, everything we had been through with it, and it might have been wrong? Once we had my diagnosis, we never considered testing Kyle because my OB-GYN placed the burden of failing to get pregnant squarely on my shoulders.

Dr. Wing saw our shock and continued. "When it comes to infertility, I see three main groups. The first is women with PCOS, endometriosis, blocked or damaged fallopian tubes, or other underlying conditions that prevent conception. That's about one-third of cases. The next third is men who have problems with their sperm or other conditions that make *them* infertile. And the last group is where we just don't know. If you look at the math, you'll see that there are some couples where both partners have something that affects their fertility."

Mary was quick to chime in with her kind voice. "It's not at all that you've done anything wrong," she said. "We just need to know exactly what we're dealing with, and that will help us give you the very best chance of getting pregnant."

It made sense, and we understood it. But it made me wish even more that we had started with an infertility specialist first or at least had both been tested early on to know what cards we were dealt. The tests were so easy and quick too: blood draws for each, a simple vaginal ultrasound for me, a sperm sample from Kyle, and in one visit we could have avoided so much heartache. I flashed back to all those failed pregnancy tests and the overwhelming sadness they caused, and suddenly saw that all along, no amount of hoping or praying would have changed their outcome. It felt like we had wasted time, and time was the one thing of which we had a limited supply.

Dr. Wing added some additional blood panels he wanted to examine, ordered a sperm sample from Kyle, and brought us into a small, dark room for an ultrasound. Here, once again, we saw my ovaries with telltale small black specks giving them the appearance of a chocolate-chip cookie. This confirmed my PCOS diagnosis, at least. To Kyle, Dr. Wing explained, "Every month, multiple immature eggs or follicles—we often use them interchangeably, but follicles are the house that holds the egg—come to the surface of Samantha's ovaries. This is different from normally functioning ovaries where one mature egg should be released. None of these follicles are of a high enough quality for conception."

Kyle asked, "Why didn't the Clomid work? Wasn't it supposed to make the eggs mature?" "Yeah," I asked, grateful Kyle brought it up as I was still confused as well. "Wasn't it supposed to make my eggs mature?" Dr. Wing said that the tests we would be doing that day would hopefully shed some light on just that question and left us in the capable hands of the lab.

While I was getting poked and prodded, Kyle was sent into a private room with a clear plastic cup, a brown paper bag, and an explanation of what he had to do. We tried to keep it mature, but we definitely snickered throughout the instructions. We kept up the banter on the way home, making a few dirty jokes that led to some dirty flirting. By the time we got to the house, I thought Kyle might need to deliver another sample, and we spent the afternoon having sex for fun for the first time in a long time. It was just what we needed.

A few days later, we found ourselves back in Dr. Wing's office, waiting for our test results and to find out the next steps. It almost felt like we had been sent to the principal and were waiting to find out just how many detentions we were going to get. Nervously, I fidgeted with my hands, wringing them and picking at my nails. My right knee bobbed up and down rapidly, burning off some of the anxiety that was building with each passing moment. Kyle noticed and took my hand in his with a reassuring smile. Shortly, the door opened and there was Dr. Wing, rushing in with a folder under his arm. He greeted us, sat behind the desk, and straightened the papers in the folder by giving them a sharp tap on his desk. Then, after a quick clearing of his throat, he began in his matter-of-fact tone.

"Samantha," he began, "as you already knew they would, the tests confirmed your PCOS. But they also showed Kyle has a very low sperm count, and there are issues with the morphology of the sperm he does have."

"I don't know what morphology means," I said. I wanted to make sure I knew exactly what was happening.

"That's basically the shape of the sperm," he explained. "If you think of a sperm, it looks like an oval with a tail. The ovals here are more triangular than they should be. Sometimes they have two heads, or no tails. Basically, they are not normal sperm."

I watched Kyle digest this out of the corner of my eye. He looked stricken, truly bothered by the fact that he had contributed to our problems without ever knowing. I tried to make him laugh, and with a big smile on my face I exclaimed, "We both suck!" He looked at me horrified for a moment, then saw the joke in my eyes and returned the grin. I reached around him and hugged him in the chair and whispered in his ear that we are always a team.

Dr. Wing pressed on with a bemused smile on his face. "Well, that's a response I've never heard before. So, with the combination of each of your underlying problems, no amount of medications or home techniques would work. The only way the two of you can conceive is with in vitro fertilization, or IVF."

I knew this was hard for Kyle to hear, but for me, an immense weight was lifted. No longer was this all my fault, my body holding the both of us back. This was something we shared now, and a burden shared is a burden lightened. I didn't even realize until that moment just how much blame I placed on myself for our failure to get pregnant. And suddenly, that blame was gone. I felt like I could breathe for the first time in months.

Dr. Wing went on to explain why, given both of our diagnoses, IVF would be our best option. Since we didn't really know what IVF was, he gave us a crash course. We would use medications to help mature my follicles. Then, in a minor surgical procedure, those eggs would be harvested and combined with Kyle's sperm in a lab. If we were successful and had viable embryos, they would then be frozen, and then later one embryo would be implanted into my uterus, where it would hopefully develop into a healthy, happy baby. This tsunami of medical procedures was not how I ever pictured our journey to parenthood, but if this was what it took to get pregnant, I was all in.

"Is this something you'd be interested in pursuing?" Dr. Wing asked.

I was scared and unclear about all of the process but would have started that second if it was possible. I felt like we had already been trying and waiting so long for a baby. But first, I wanted to make sure Kyle was as gung ho as I was. We said that we would be interested in getting more information about it without making a commitment. He brought us to Mary, who was in a smaller, brighter office decorated with warm colors that complemented her personality. She patiently went through the process in greater detail, rattling off an intimidating list of medications with names longer than winter in Chicago. She talked about success rates, what to expect emotionally and physically, and then took time to answer the many questions Kyle and I had. Even so, it felt like we didn't have enough information to ask the right questions or even know what the right questions were. Mary gave us a pile of pamphlets and brochures and resources to review at home. She then had us meet with a representative of REACH's financial department, but had a piece of advice for us before taking us to that office.

"You're going to have questions, and that's totally normal. When you want to know something, *call me*. Don't fall down the rabbit hole of the internet. So much of it is not accurate, or not representative of what nearly everyone experiences. I promise I'll always answer your questions honestly and as accurately as I'm able."

I felt like she was already in my head, knowing how I work. She brought us down the hall to another small but functional office where the financial representative was waiting. When we learned the cost of IVF, we just about fell out of our seats. Now, I know just how blessed we are. Kyle and I have the financial resources to be able to afford IVF, but even in that moment as we were learning how expensive this was going to be, I wondered how people who did not have the resources would have been able to afford it at all. It was a staggering amount of money, and it was broken down into treatment schedules and payment deadlines and a thick packet of papers detailing it all. The thought of other people giving up at this point sat heavy on my heart.

We were mostly silent on the hour-long drive home, drifting in oceans of information and swirling in whirlpools of emotion. Fear, excitement, uncertainty, relief, and elation all fought for dominance. Kyle added in some of the guilt that I had just released, processing for the first time his own biological issues that we did not know about before today. But we were in it together, and even in our separate silences, we held hands along the highway, connected one to the other in our places of thought and reflection.

After dinner, I ignored Mary's advice and went to my thinking place with my laptop. Since I was a kid, when I needed to work out a thorny problem, I brought a pillow into the bathroom to place against the wall. I would sit on the cool tile floor and research until I knew how I felt about something. This night was no different. I spent hours on that floor with a small space heater blowing warm air, clicking through article after article, each one more horrifying than the next. Some of the stories that I read were horrifying, but others were deeply inspiring. When I was done, I knew there was nothing I wouldn't risk to have a child of my own.

And so, at two-thirty in the morning, from the cool tile floor of my now-too-hot bathroom, I emailed REACH and asked them to set an appointment. I told Kyle the next morning, and he was relieved. He hadn't wanted to pressure me either way, but it was clear now that this was the decision he wanted too. "I'll be with you every step of the way," he said. "There's nothing we can't do together."

A few days later we were again back at REACH, and this time Mary walked us through the nitty-gritty. She also added another piece of extremely simple advice that I try to follow to this day: "Take it one step at a time," she said. "If you start jumping ahead to procedures coming up or worrying about the embryo transfer before you even collect your eggs, you are going to stress yourself out more in an already stressful situation."

I opened my notebook, and after flipping past numerous pages of questions and notes, with broad strokes across the top, I wrote, "One step at a time." I knew I was going to have to make this my mantra to get through the next months, and I also knew it wasn't going to be easy. I thrive in the details; I relish planning out every last twist and turn. Here, I was going to have to be present and let God and the medical professionals handling my care manage the details. It would be an exercise in patience, and in a whole new form of self-discipline. I closed the notebook and indicated that Mary should continue.

It turned out that most of her presentation was devoted to training us on how to manage the at-home medical work we were going to have to do. "The first thing you'll need to know," she said, "is how to administer the shots."

"I hate shots. You might hear me say that and think, 'Samantha doesn't like shots,' but I need you to hear me. I. Hate. Shots."

She laughed and went through a series of medications we'd have to give in a specific order and in precise doses. With each medicine, she brought out a syringe with a gleaming silver needle attached to its end. And with every needle, I felt closer and closer to passing out. "Can't we give these in pills?" I asked, trying to push down the panic.

"I'm sorry, Samantha. Every patient wishes there were pills available. I wish there were too. But shots are a huge part of the process."

I paled and started taking slow, deep breaths to try and calm myself. I *hate* shots. As a kid, I pulled a Houdini and escaped from an exam room to avoid getting a vaccine. When I need blood drawn, they have to bring out the tiniest baby needle. When I need a finger stick, they physically have to hold my hand down and pin my finger. I cry every single time. Not so much during it but before it even happens. It's that anticipation that kills me. And here I was needing a daily routine of shots. Maybe this was a bad idea.

Mary quickly explained that I would not be giving myself the shots and directed the bulk of her instruction at Kyle. I tried to go to my happy place, picturing our Caribbean hideaway with the bright blue salt water washing warmly up on shining white beaches. The sound of the blood rushing in my ears nearly matched the gentle roar of the Caribbean Sea. It didn't totally work, but it kept me from running for the hills. "One step at a time," I told myself. "This is how you get your baby."

As I visualized, Mary laid out an array of torture devices on the desk in front of her and handed Kyle an orange on which to practice injections. My knee started its furious bobbing again, and with every stab, I swooned, quickly correcting Kyle on his techniques. Like I knew anything. "It's not going to be so bad, babe," he said. I looked at him like he was nuts. "NOT THAT BAD?" I shrieked, pointing at the armory of menacing needles spread out in front of us. "I HAVE TO HAVE THOSE EVERY DAY!"

He calmly looked me in the eye, pulled up his shirt, pinched an inch of skin, and quickly grabbed a practice needle and plunged it into his own belly.

"See?"

"Kyle!" I couldn't believe it. He was sitting there in front of me, a giant needle sticking out of his stomach with a *smile* on his face. My husband was insane. But insane in a "knight in shining armor" kind of way, which was exactly what I needed right then.

"I've never seen a husband do that before," said Mary as she retrieved the needle and put a small, round Band-Aid over the puncture. "But don't ever take a needle that isn't sterile and jab yourself with it again, Kyle." He laughed and promised he wouldn't but bragged about how he was a pro already.

"You've given one shot in your entire life, and you gave it to yourself and you're a *pro*?" I married a madman. A cocky, loveable madman.

A few days later, we found ourselves driving home from the pharmacy with two big brown bags of medicines and supplies. I was really nervous. I'm someone who doesn't even like to take an Advil for a headache, and here I was about to be jabbed with a series of needles at home so that in a couple of weeks a doctor could take another needle to pierce my ovaries and suck out my eggs. My recent experiences with Clomid left me anxious about medications and their side effects. My mind kept circling around the idea of this not working, and what we would do then. But underneath the anxieties it was a bubbling excitement, a clear spring of hope bursting up, knowing that if this ended up with a baby, it would all be worth it. *One step at a time,* I reminded myself.

That evening Kyle cleared the kitchen counter and, like a mad scientist, began to lay out the collection of medicines and syringes that would make my eggs grow. He had a crazed grin on his face, and it looked like he was actually *enjoying* this. I badgered him about every little detail, making sure he was consulting and marking each medicine on the color-coded calendar I made in a fit of OCD mania. Fat, hot tears splashed on the kitchen floor as I paced back and forth, trying to talk myself into it. With each word, my pitch got higher and higher until it was probably only the dogs who could hear.

"You ready, honey?" Kyle said, a syringe in one hand and an alcohol wipe in the other.

"No," I said. I was *not* ready for my own personal Dr. McDreamy to start stabbing me in my own house. "I changed my mind; we don't need to do this." I was starting to hyperventilate.

He guided me to the couch, and I panicked. Spots swam in my vision, and my breath came in short, harsh gasps. I was afraid I was going to pass out. Distantly, I felt Kyle pinch the skin of my belly as he got ready to administer the shot, and I snapped to alertness, great gusts of panic blowing through my soul. "I'm not ready," I tried to say, but I'm not sure if anyone could have heard it. And then it was over. The first shot was a quick, sharp sting, which faded quickly. The second hurt more because Kyle struggled with getting the delivery pen to operate at first, but even that was not nearly as bad as the anticipation of it.

I let out a little chuckle as Kyle collapsed exhausted onto the couch next to me.

"What are you laughing about?" he asked, puzzled. With tears carrying dark rivers of mascara down my cheeks, I sheepishly replied that it really wasn't that bad at all. I was a little embarrassed about the theatrics, but only a little. After all, my husband had just viciously stabbed me in the stomach with two wicked needles. He rolled his eyes in mock exasperation and wrapped me up in a huge bear hug. We both felt like we had been through an ordeal, but we were now on our way.

13

NEEDLES, NEEDLES EVERYWHERE

It's amazing how quickly you can adapt to a new routine. Our formerly pristine, beautiful kitchen was now a medical laboratory, with piles of individually wrapped syringes, needles in their protective hard plastic cases, medication bottles lined up one after the other. Where there used to be healthy olive oils and neat piles of garlic and a bottle of nice white wine that I used for cooking, there were now boxes of gauze squares and alcohol wipes. And high in our cupboard, perched on the shelf above our cereal bowls, was a red plastic bin to collect used needles, a reminder every morning that this was a new way of life for us.

As we prepared to administer my shots each evening, I found some humor in the situation even though I was still nervous. This had been such a difficult time, but together we managed to find humor and joy inside the pain. We planned, we laughed, and we worked together in love.

Once again, I had turned to Dr. Google for strategies on how to master all the new skills we were developing. I learned that with this process came bloating, and that I should drink lots of water. So, I turned my ever-present water bottle into a concoction the best spas in the world would have been proud to offer, with bits of cut-up fruit and delicious spices like ginger or mint adding flavor and nutrients as I sipped. One of the many tips out there suggested that organization was key, and we already know I can put Martha Stewart to shame with my organizing skills. I sorted the syringes and needles and medications by type and order and ease of access, which gave me a feeling of being back in control. Hope quietly crept back into my heart after a long absence. I was no longer aimless, flailing, and grasping at any possible technique. We had real diagnoses, a real doctor, and real medicine. I'd found purpose in the middle of all the madness.

At night, Kyle and I laughed and made jokes as we got ready for the shots.

"Nurse, give me a twenty-four-gauge needle," he'd say with a rakish grin.

"Here you are, doctor," I replied, handing him a hard plastic tube, open at one end, ready for him to screw it onto the threads at the end of the syringe. He'd draw up the medicine, hold up the clear plastic syringe, and tap the air bubbles to the top before carefully pressing the plunger until the tiniest bead of liquid glistened at its top. He would then gently pinch the skin of my belly, jab me with the needle, and inject me with the medicine as I tried not to scream, squirm, or run away.

We rotated my injection sites night by night, hoping to avoid getting too sore—although we always avoided the agony of the space directly beneath my belly button, which seemed to alleviate the pain of the needle prick some. It also reduced the bruising and made the medicines sting less when they went in. Before and after each shot, I would apply ice packs to keep the swelling down and numb the pain. Before long, it felt like second nature.

Now, that's not to say we didn't have our mishaps. One night a few days into the process Kyle gave me a shot, and afterward some of the medicine leaked out of the puncture. Frantically, he and I tried without success to coax and push and press the leaking medicine back into the near-microscopic pinprick left by the needle. Not knowing whether we should inject more medicine or if we had really screwed things up, I called the on-call nurse at REACH. She assured us that a small amount of medicine leaking out one night would not make a difference, and suggested we do a few things to keep it from happening again. This became our go-to technique, and we used it after that. First, we would pinch my skin and the fat just beneath it into a roll. Quickly and firmly inject the needle, and slowly but at a steady pace inject the medicine. After it's all in, we'd hold the needle in place, count to four, release the roll of skin, and remove the needle. *Voila!* No more leaks.

On day five, we had to add another shot into the mix. I was less than thrilled about this one because Dr. Google had some harsh things to say about the medicine. I was extremely anxious about the whole thing, which of course made Kyle anxious. It was starting to get difficult to find a good injection site that hadn't been used. It didn't help that this medicine required a bigger needle, or that it felt like being bitten by a fire ant when it went in and the burning of the medicine kept going for about fifteen minutes. After the shot, Kyle stroked my hair as I cried into his lap. We were both a bit frazzled by the experience and needed a moment to just feel connected to each other. The next morning, there was significantly more bruising than there had been before, but like all women on this brutal journey, I was tough. I could take it.

Despite our nightly regimen, we had our lives to continue. We still spent weekends at racetracks, Kyle and I kept doing media appearances, and mostly we had to pretend we weren't a walking Walgreens. Late in the first week, nausea set in; it's one of the side effects of the drug cocktails. Like I would later experience with morning sickness, this started as just aversions to foods like apples. Eventually, it morphed into an all-day quea-siness with occasional spikes of "Oh my God, I'm going to puke," although it never actually got that far.

One of these days we were walking down the pit road at a racetrack. It was hot, with heat shimmering off the asphalt and hundreds of people crowded around me and I was certain I was going to hurl. Frantic, I looked around for a place to vomit, and came up empty. A garbage can, with all these people watching? The porta potties? Nope, no, I was not getting my face anywhere close to the toilet in one of those. I eyed Kyle's racecar and wondered what would happen if I puked in there. How gross would that be for Kyle? Then I remembered: after the race, his team took care of the car, and I didn't want *them* to have to clean up my mess. Maybe I could blame it on Kyle! And suddenly, just as it was about to happen, the nausea passed. A fan tapped me on the shoulder and asked me for a selfie. I turned and smiled, swallowed hard against the putrid lump in my throat, and wiped the beads of sweat off my forehead as the nausea subsided.

Another nasty side effect of all these medications and the hormones they stimulated was extreme exhaustion. As the days progressed toward my egg retrieval, I felt like I was trudging through chest-deep water everywhere I went. Everything was an effort, and when this overwhelming fatigue was combined with the nausea, I felt pretty terrible most of the time. I spent the majority of my days curled into a fetal position on the cool floor of the pantry, eating the one thing I could stomach without wanting to throw up: Nacho Cheese Doritos. I was back in my pity party, wondering why I had to suffer this much just to have a baby. I thought about how unfair it seemed that other people have accidental babies while we had been trying for so long already that we should have a toddler crawling on the floor I was now lying on. I knew I was not going to feel physically great during this process, but this was so much worse than I expected.

After a couple of days of feeling this way, I called my nurse again at REACH, who asked me to come in a day earlier than planned to get some bloodwork. It wasn't long before we got the results and learned that my estrogen levels were much higher than we thought they'd be, and that this was the culprit behind how I was feeling. What a relief that was, learning that it was something we could manage, and that it wouldn't be weeks upon weeks of feeling this way. She adjusted dosing on some of the meds, and quickly I started to feel better. The nausea lifted, and I could eat more than junk food and started to regain some energy.

On the eighth day of the shots, my ovaries were very swollen—especially the one on the right. It looked like a plump almond trying to pop out of my skin when I laid flat, and I was feeling very bloated. Inside, it was almost as though I could feel my ovaries swelling like little water balloons attached to a hose, and I hoped they were filling with mature, usable eggs. I wanted this to work so badly, and I was overly aware of every little detail of my body, hyper-analyzing every feeling. Another part of this whole ordeal is that I had to keep a clear calendar for all of the appointments that I had, and that day was no exception. I was due at REACH, and despite having planned for nine to twelve days of shots and then receiving a trigger shot to get the eggs ready to harvest, the doctor wanted us to administer the trigger shot that night. A quick ultrasound and new bloodwork showed that my eggs were the correct size already. This was a huge milestone for us, as it meant that in less than two days, they would be retrieving my eggs!

Throughout all this, men have an extremely important role to play besides shot-giver, hair-stroker, pharmacist, therapist, and chauffeur. Yep, Kyle's sperm was the other half of the equation. And while what the male partners in infertility go through physically is less than what we women bear, it's important to remember that they also are going through it. Psychologically, men often struggle with the idea of problems with their sperm. Kyle was diagnosed with a low sperm count, and many of his sperm were misshapen. Before all this, I didn't even know that was a thing, but they can have heads that are too flat or too pointy. Sometimes they can even have two heads, which doesn't lead to twins, but to no babies at all. It felt like a bad 1950s sci-fi movie: *The Sperm with Two Heads!*

Given that we both had biological issues with fertility, it felt like it all evened out for him. The issues with his sperm did not affect him physically or psychologically on a daily basis the way my PCOS did. But he did confide in me that if our problems with getting pregnant had been solely related to the issues with his sperm, he would have felt extremely guilty watching me go through everything I'd had to endure on his account. I reassured him that we were a team, and that any problem one of us had was a problem that both of us had—not just in fertility but in life. Being open and honest about how we were each feeling really helped us get through the hardest of these times.

Of course, not all of these times were hard.

Kyle needed to go in and make his sperm donation. During an earlier visit, our sweet nurse Mary had run down the collection process with us. Kyle would be given a specimen cup and a "gentleman's magazine" and sent alone into a small private room to collect his semen. How to get that semen was left up to him, but we both got the picture.

As the day came close, I realized the gentleman's magazine bothered me. There was no way in hell I was having him look at another woman while getting our baby sperm! This whole situation is sterile and awkward enough, but I would be damned if some Playmate was the inspiration behind this particular sample. This had to be an act of love—it was the baby sperm!

I told Kyle this, and he looked at me like I had two heads (you know, like his wacky sperm).

"Sam," he said, "I've got to look at something. It's weird to go in that room and try to make this happen without something to help."

He was right, and so I came up with a plan.

One day when Kyle was out, I made myself look really good, putting on my reddest lipstick, my thickest mascara, and my skimpiest lingerie. I started taking pictures.

I was alone in the room, setting up my camera on a timer, trying to take the sexiest photos I could imagine. I lay across the bed. I vamped in front of the mirror. I came up with camera angles and poses that would make any sketchy adult film studio in the San Fernando Valley jealous.

Soon, the lingerie started to come off.

I really didn't want Kyle thinking of another woman when he deposited our baby sperm. In fact, if these pictures turned out half as hot as I hoped they would, I didn't think he'd look at any woman ever again. It turned out that not all of my infertility hormones were bad for Kyle.

As we drove to the clinic for Kyle's date with himself, and for me to be knocked out and have my eggs sucked out through a giant needle in my vagina, I realized Kyle was going to be having a much better day than I was. I sent the best of the pictures to his phone. When Mary handed him the cup, I told him to check his texts.

He gave me a look.

I gave him a wink, and a secret smile.

It didn't take Kyle very long at all to collect his sample. He came out with a self-satisfied grin on his face and a paper bag that held our baby sperm in a plastic cup.

"I guess I didn't need that magazine after all," he said. We were almost there. Next stop? Collecting my eggs.

14

EXCEEDING EGGSPECTATIONS

A day or two before my eggs were retrieved, my mother had popped by to help us out around the yard. She and Pops moved to North Carolina a few years after Kyle and I got married, and I can't begin to tell you what a big help they were. They were semiretired and were always looking for projects. As she was weeding in the front yard, a bright flash of white glinted between the blades of grass, half buried in the rich brown soil beneath a bush. Curious, she dug it up, brushed off the dirt, and revealed an antique baby boy figurine, with bright blue eyes and chubby red cheeks. Holding it in her hands, she instantly felt Grandma's presence filling her with a sense of calm in her otherwise anxious nerves. She was so committed to this working for us, to seeing her daughter become a mother, and she believed with all her heart that this was a sign from her own mother, left to reassure us.

The peace and happiness this brought to us is hard to explain, but it was truly meaningful. If you've ever lost someone, you know the hollow places in your life that absence creates. Years later, you find yourself still wanting to talk to them when big events happen, or even little events that bring back memories. Scents, the sound of wind chimes, the taste of hot black coffee in a thick mug could remind you of the empty space they used to occupy. And with Kyle and I having been through so much and about to take our next steps on this journey, I felt my grandmother's absence everywhere. This little doll filled in some of that hollow space and made me feel connected to her in a whole new way.

It was with this happy find in our hearts that we left for REACH bright and early on my egg retrieval day. This was a surgical procedure, where I would be anesthetized and in a deep sleep while my medical team would collect eggs from my ripened ovaries and prepare them for fertilization. Neither Kyle nor I are morning people, but for this predawn wakeup we were wide-eyed and vibrating with nervous energy.

Upon arrival at REACH, a friendly receptionist greeted us warmly and escorted us into a small curtained room with a pair of chairs. She had me sign enough paperwork to make me think I was applying for a mortgage, and as she presented me with a cotton hospital gown with small silver snaps in the back and a bright blue hairnet, Mary arrived. She gave me a huge hug and smiled with such genuine warmth that any worries I had about the procedure melted like spring snowflakes. She talked me through what would be happening again, even though I knew it by heart at this point. Dr. Wing and his team would attempt to collect as many eggs as they could from my ovaries. She cautioned me that just because they harvested an egg, it didn't mean that it would be of high enough quality to fertilize, and not all the eggs we did end up fertilizing would make viable embryos. She let me know that I'd feel a little bit foggy when I woke up from the anesthesia, and that while I might be a little bit nauseated, they would be giving me medicine during the procedure to keep this to a minimum. I was more afraid of going under and never waking up, the thought of a needle puncturing my ovaries, and the possibility that none of my eggs were of good enough quality to fertilize.

She gave me a minute to change into the gown, pop the hairnet over my messy bun, and put on the lilac-hued fuzzy socks I brought especially for this procedure. Purple was my grandmother's favorite color, and given my mom finding her "omen" in the yard, I wanted to bring her colorful spirit with me today. Then it was time.

"They're ready for you in the operating room," Mary said, popping her head into the room. Kyle gave me a kiss, told me he'd be right there when I woke up, and placed his hand across the small of my back. I never wanted him to let go and wished he could be there in the operating room with me, but it was for the best that only the medical team was allowed there. And I was off, slowly shuffling down the tiled hallway, Mary leading the way.

When I arrived in the operating room, which was unexpectedly decorated with a childlike sea life mural, I tightly smiled at the team and moved over to the table. A nurse wrapped a blood pressure cuff around my right arm, and on the index finger of my left hand she placed a beige plastic clip that would make sure I was getting enough oxygen. She started an IV in the same hand and connected it to a large bag of clear fluid hanging from a nearby metal pole. Soon she was putting what seemed like a million stickers on my chest to measure my heart rate and breathing during the procedure. Dr. Wing and the anesthesiologist walked in, and he exclaimed that it was going to be a good day. Someone asked me to scoot down the table and gently placed my legs into the stirrups. This is when panic started to set in. I knew stories of people waking up during surgery and being unable to move or communicate even though they could feel everything. I heard the anesthesiologist say, "Okay, she's looking a little nervous. Samantha, I promise you we're going to take such good care of you. Let's get started." Then somebody started pushing a large syringe full of white liquid into the IV, and I was out.

I blinked and saw the fuzzy outline of Kyle's face looking down at me. At least, I thought it was Kyle. I couldn't see a darn thing, and I was having a hard time concentrating on anything.

"Kyle?" I asked, my throat scratchy and dry.

"I'm here, babe. You took longer than we thought to wake up!"

"I can't see you. How many eggs did they get?"

"I haven't seen the doctors yet, so I'm not sure." He handed me my glasses, and his relieved face came into sharper focus. My mind didn't though. I think a nurse came in and took my vitals, and I think Kyle asked her if she had any news. She told us the doctor would be in to see us soon, and I fell back asleep.

The next thing I knew, Kyle was shaking me awake to let me know Dr. Wing was there. I blinked hard to clear the sleep from my eyes and the anesthesia haze from my mind. My belly was sore, and I could feel that while I slept, someone had put a heating pad on it. I saw Dr. Wing, and he looked happy. My heart started to flutter excitedly, but I was still out of it, and it was hard to focus.

"You did great, Samantha," he said. "We collected thirty-four eggs."

I was overjoyed with the results, but Dr. Wing was quick to remind me that this number would probably shrink dramatically. Not all these eggs would be usable, he reiterated. Even so, Kyle was so excited that he and I posed for a selfie, my glazed eyes staring zombie-like at the camera. He coaxed me into holding my fingers up in a three and a four to show how many eggs we had.

I was starting to feel bloated and tired, and just wanted to go home and rest in my own bed. Soon, the medical staff declared me fit for travel, and we were on our way. I slept most of the ride home, and when I woke, I was feeling even more bloated. I took some pain medicine, wrapped myself in soft blankets, and dozed on the couch as the TV flickered in front of me. Soon I went to bed, where I slept straight through the night.

When I woke the next morning, I was feeling even more swollen and sore. The pain medications and anesthesia had really backed me up (and totally worn off), and all I wanted to do was use the bathroom. Even with the gentle laxatives the REACH team had recommended, that seemed like it was not going to happen. A quick hop on the scale revealed I had gained six pounds since the previous morning. It was a shitty time, pun intended.

I also noticed a faint rash on my stomach, which was uncomfortably itchy. Grumpily, I stomped off to the kitchen to find anything with massive amounts of fiber. I spent the morning sitting on the toilet staring at my phone, waiting for *something* to happen. Nothing did. The phone didn't ring. The constipation didn't let up. The only thing going on was my itchy stomach and my curdling mood. I was literally taking shots of liquid laxatives to wash down laxative tablets, definitely not the best cocktail I'd ever had.

Finally, in the late afternoon, my phone lit up with the REACH phone number. I ran out to Kyle so we could answer it together. Excitedly, we asked how we did. Of the thirty-four eggs collected, a whopping *fifteen* had been fertilized. Even though we were again cautioned that we'd lose some embryos in the coming days, we were overjoyed—we honestly didn't know if we'd end up with any. Due to the issues with Kyle's sperm, an embryologist directly injected Kyle's sperm into my eggs using a process called *intracytoplasmic sperm injection* (ICSI) instead of putting the eggs and sperm together and letting nature take its course, as if anything at all was natural about this. It was all about as natural as Froot Loops.

It would be a few days until the embryos were sent off to genetic testing, and before hanging up the nurse promised to keep us updated on the embryo count if it changed. Kyle and I had agonized over whether to do this testing or not—it's morally complicated. We didn't want to take a glimpse into the unknown and let it steer our decision, and we certainly didn't want to make decisions based on biological factors, but we also desperately wanted to have the best chance of a successful pregnancy. What ultimately swayed us was that Dr. Wing explained genetic testing could reduce the risk of a miscarriage. I didn't know if I could take that after all we had been through—I thought it might break me beyond repair—and so we opted for the test.

After thanking the nurse, we hung up the phone and whooped and hollered and hugged and danced around the kitchen as much as my bloated and backed-up body would allow. Fifteen embryos gave us so many chances at making this work.

The next day, I was so uncomfortable that I called my mom, who had been a nurse for twenty-five years. She said that there is a particular laxative, which colonoscopy patients are given over ice, and thirty minutes later anything inside them is on its way out. This sounded like my kind of fix, and so I got dressed to head out to the drugstore. As I was changing, I saw my swollen belly in the mirror, and couldn't help but wonder if this was what I would look like pregnant. I turned this way and that, my hand over the bulge, and imagined it was. I put on the tightest top I had, unconsciously—okay, very consciously—hoping that when I went out, other people would also think I was pregnant.

I got to the pharmacy and uncomfortably started searching the laxatives for the brand my mom recommended. As I browsed, an elderly woman came up to me and asked me what I was having. My heart raced! This is what it would be like!

"We're keeping it a surprise," I lied. I knew I shouldn't have, but I *really* didn't want to explain that I was hoping to have a poop baby very soon. I also didn't want to make her feel bad for assuming. But mostly, I wanted to live out this fantasy of being recognized as a mother. We chatted amiably for a few minutes, and she wished me and my baby well. I smiled just a little guiltily and thanked her for her kind words.

As she departed, my eyes spied the bright yellow bottle on the shelf that Mom had suggested. Thinking of the interaction I just had, and not wanting this to progress until I looked eight months pregnant, I bought two and raced home. An hour later I no longer looked pregnant.

Over the next couple of days, we got news that we were down to eleven viable embryos, and they would be sent off for genetic testing. This process would take a few days, which Kyle and I spent as nervous wrecks. Every morning and night, we would pray to have at least one healthy embryo. We realized just how much hope we had invested in this process, and worried that it was all for nothing. Kyle and I spent a lot of time lost in our own thoughts, sitting together on the couch holding hands and staring at nothing on the TV. We were in purgatory, with both heaven and hell staring us down with closed gates.

Before too long the call came. After genetic testing, we still had eight embryos! We were thrilled. When the nurse asked if we wanted to know the genders, we both nearly shouted YES! into the phone. "You have five boys and three girls," she said. Overwhelmed, we thanked the nurse profusely and hung up. I tackled Kyle on the couch and covered him with kisses. We locked eyes, and he shouted "BOY!" without me even asking. We laughed, but we also needed to talk about it.

Ultimately, after laying out pros and cons, we decided on a boy first and a girl second. As you know by now, we're both planners, and this was our time to shine. A younger sister to keep him honest and kind, and an older brother to always be there to protect her. And she would be there to cheer him on racing and probably end up dating his friends. We thought it was the perfect plan. Based on the results of the genetic testing, the fifth boy embryo was graded the best. Our choice was made. Dr. Wing said he wanted to wait a month to do the transfer. He'd had the best success with frozen transfers, he said, because it gave the mother's body time to recover from the egg retrieval and all the hormone injections.

That month was bliss. It was just the break my body and mind needed before starting on a pregnancy journey. I took this time to do all the high-intensity workouts, sushi eating, champagne drinking, and trampoline jumping my little heart desired. Kyle and I went out on dates and had nights out with friends. I felt like my old self, my pre-infertility Samantha, coming back into her body and getting ready to be a mother.

I was ready.

15

BABY FINALLY ON BOARD

Some couples have fantasies about playing doctor. Well, once you've had to actually play doctor at home, the fantasy dies . . . forever. From shots, medications, and patches to the thick, goopy gel I had to put way up where the sun doesn't shine, we learned a whole new set of skills as quickly as we could, and none of it was sexy or fun.

Here was our routine. After breakfast, I took doxycyline, an antibiotic that reduces the risk of bacterial infection during the transfer, along with a prenatal vitamin big enough for an elephant mama and a baby Tylenol. Next, I had to apply Crinone. This is a progesterone gel, and yep, it goes in your vagina. While I was glad it wasn't another shot, I sure didn't love it, as it reminded me of checking my vaginal mucus thickness—but it was super easy. It comes in its own syringe, and you just squirt it on up in there. I learned pretty quickly to always wear a pad, as it seemed to have a habit of gushing back out at the least opportune times. Gross. But at least it didn't hurt at all, and unlike the mucus it didn't turn me off to egg whites. Bonus.

That first night, we started the progesterone in oil shots. My poor butt.

One of the things you have to do when getting ready to transfer an embryo into its new uterine home is thicken up the lining of your uterus. The way you do that? Progesterone in oil shots. In your butt. A whole lot of them. Now, as you all know by now, I am a huge baby when it comes to needles. And of course, I had visited Dr. Google and read up on them beforehand, which just took my anxiety to a whole new level. It was like reading a series of Yelp reviews about torture techniques.

"Literally a pain in the butt," one woman wrote.

"Feels like you've been kicked in the ass. Hard," wrote another.

"Massive bruising: 0/5 stars."

"The most painful part of the whole process."

I was getting panicky, so I called Mary at REACH again to see if I could talk my way out of getting the injections. "First of all, Samantha," she said, "I know you. I ordered you smaller needles because the normal needles will freak you out. These will take a bit longer to administer the injection because the oil is thick, but the shot and the aftereffects will be *way* less painful than you're reading."

Smaller needles? They make smaller needles; why didn't anybody tell me this before?

"Next," she said, "go down to your pharmacy and pick up the box of lidocaine patches I just called in for you. Pop one on half an hour before your shots, and you'll be nice and numb. Then you can warm up the oil a little before the shots by holding it in your hands or wrapping a warm towel around it. This will make it thinner and easier to inject."

I liked the idea of warm oil. I was trying to think of this as a little daily butt massage now instead of my husband sadistically stabbing me with a giant dripping torture implement.

"Use a fast motion just like before, quickly poke the upper corner of your butt, and slowly but consistently push the oil in."

She was harshing my massage mellow.

"And then afterward, always massage the area for five to ten minutes. This will work the medicine in, and also reduce bruising."

Ahh. Back in massage bliss.

Maybe it was the extra padding in my butt compared to my stomach, but when we finally got to administering these shots, they didn't bother me at all early on. I had some mild bruising and was a little bit sore, but it wasn't bad. Later, after getting pregnant, I had to stay on them for about ten weeks, and my butt did get pretty beat up from an extra seventy days of shots, but these first days were so much easier than I expected.

Over time we learned how to set everything up together in the most efficient ways for us. I wouldn't exactly call it fun; it was something we did together as a team, adding a new level of intimacy to our relationship. It also gave us a few laughs, like the time we snuck off to the bathroom together during a corporate dinner, leaving everyone thinking we had snuck off for a quickie. Or the quick shot in the back seat of a car, where another couple in the lot thought we were getting it on. I wish our sex life had been this spontaneous during all of this, but alas, it was all for the shots.

So much of every day leading up to this had been work. We woke up to shots and pain and crazy schedules and hormones, and today we woke up to the possibility of getting pregnant. There was so much riding on the day, and I'd be lying if I said I didn't feel that pressure, but we tried hard to tamp it down. We wanted our baby to be transferred into a joyous, calm womb.

After arriving at the clinic, we were escorted into the same curtained room we had been in weeks before for our egg retrieval. This time, there were gowns and ridiculous blue bouffant caps that would keep our hair contained laid out for both of us. We laughed together as we helped each other into them and as I arranged Kyle's hat like a beret. We snapped pictures to remember the day, and it did almost feel like a vacation snapshot. We were somewhere we had never been before, not physically but existentially. We were transitioning out of the state of being just the two of us and into the three of us. It was intoxicating.

Tyl, our embryologist, rapped on the door and let himself in. "Your embryo warmed nicely this morning," he said with a smile. His teal scrubs went perfectly with his name, and I smiled back. His expert hands had injected Kyle's sperm into my egg, and it almost felt like he was part of the family as a result. He told us our embryo was dividing as expected and handed us a picture. While all we saw was a clump of bubble-looking cells, tears still filled our eyes and the nurses let out happy *oohs* and *aahs* as they looked over our shoulders at our son. As I looked at this strange little picture, I could see his future mapping out already. I could hear his voice saying "Mama" for the first time, with Kyle's mischievous eyes and my dark hair. It was surreal to know he was in a catheter just a few feet away, and soon he would be inside my womb. I felt like my womb was aching for him to be tucked safe inside his home where he was meant to be.

As I settled onto the table, with my legs up in the stirrups most women know very well, I started giggling, and that giggle built into a full-on, laugh-out-loud fit. "What's so funny?" a bemused Kyle asked.

"Well, most of the time to make a baby, a couple makes love alone. But to get me pregnant, you're the *only person in the room* who doesn't get anywhere near my vagina today!"

This got the whole room going.

It was true that there was no spontaneity, no romance, no music. Soft candlelight was replaced with the harsh, bright, white fluorescents shining down from the ceiling, and the even-brighter light from the operating lamp over the table. Instead of rose petals there were shiny medical implements around the room, and the sharp scent of disinfectant in the air, and a bunch of near-strangers were standing around watching. It certainly wasn't how we had imagined this going in those early days after our wedding. But it was still *our* baby, and today was his day.

We decided to say a prayer together, to share a moment of tranquility and connection in the middle of the organized chaos. I felt Kyle take my hand in his, rubbing his thumb across the back of my hand, and I was transported back to the hundreds of prayers Kyle and I had said together—how we had begged God for a baby, how I had screamed and yelled at Him in frustration and anguish, and finally surrendered to the process, knowing God's will was behind it all. I stared at the ceiling, and while I still wondered why we had been forced to endure this trial, I also felt a flutter in my heart thinking that it was as if God was reminding me to trust in Him and His plan, and that His reasons were real even if I couldn't see them right then.

It was the loud snap of Dr. Wing pulling on his gloves that brought me back to the present. "Ready?" he asked. Kyle and I locked eyes, and the nervous excitement practically sparked in the room.

"Yes," he said.

"We're so ready," I said at the same time.

Dr. Wing explained that he was getting the catheter ready. This was the highway that our baby would be taking from outside my body to inside my womb. It involves a very full bladder, and I was surprised once again that I was not at all embarrassed to be in this position, legs open to the world and a pee pad like the one I used to train my dog, Lucy, underneath me. It was one of my first acts of motherhood, and I will never feel shame in being a mother.

"Look behind you," Dr. Wing said. I turned my head to the right, straining slightly to see over my shoulder where a shimmering black-and-white ultrasound image was projected onto a large white screen. I could see Kyle in profile, his eyes wide in excited anticipation. I was so proud to be here with him, knowing the kind of father he would be. I loved him more in that moment than maybe ever before.

"I'm inserting the first catheter now," Dr. Wing said, and as he did, the image on the screen changed and twirled as the long plastic tube snaked into my uterus. Once it was in place, a technician handed him a second, narrower catheter—the one that held our baby. Dr. Wing inserted it into the first tube and began a slow countdown. My mind was drifting through memories and hopes.

"Three."

I was back at the beginning with Kyle, legs tucked beneath me on the bed in my small undergraduate apartment, sounds of parties washing past me while I got to know the man who would become my husband.

"Two."

I was on the bathroom floor, bleeding, crying, surrounded by stick after stick telling me I was ovulating while my body refused to get pregnant.

"One."

I was decades in the future, watching my full-grown son, healthy and happy, introduce my husband to his first granddaughter. He wore the same expression of awe and pride and hope and fierce love that Kyle was wearing right at that moment.

"Go."

I was back on the table, watching the ultrasound projected onto a screen. There was a flash of white as our baby went from *outside* to *inside*. I imagined him flipping and twisting and twirling, laughing through a mouth that was not yet formed but that I already knew as well as my own. A nurse whisked the catheter away to the adjacent lab to be inspected. "Okay," said Dr. Wing, "now we wait while they see how we did. Stay very still while we check." The room was silent, and nobody moved. We patiently waited while the tube was inspected under the microscope and then from another room, we heard someone say, "All clear." That was it. It almost felt anticlimactic, as though there should have been a fundamental change in me the moment it happened, or at least balloons and confetti or something. It was such a monumental moment and in the blink of an eye it was over, and at least physically, I felt no different than I did before.

I was wheeled out of the procedure room where Mary was waiting. She told me to lie still in bed for half an hour and then we could head home.

"That's it?" I asked. "Shouldn't I be under observation? What if we hit bumpy roads on the way home? Or an accident? Shouldn't I be hooked up to monitors?" She smiled knowingly and said that I just needed to take it easy for a few days. We spent that half an hour excitedly texting the grandparents-to-be, letting them know that everything went well, and we would soon be discharged. I found my hand moving of its own accord to rest protectively over my belly.

"You can get dressed and head on home," she said. She admonished Kyle to drive like a normal person and not a NASCAR driver and said she would see us in twelve days for a blood test to see how things were progressing. In a daze, I shuffled to the car, terrified of the slightest jolt. As he backed out of the parking space and put the car in drive, he hit a tiny pothole. "Kyle! Be careful!" I shouted. Around every twist and turn, I let out protective squeaks, on every straightaway I told him to slow down. "Samantha, I'm driving five miles an hour *under* the speed limit," he said.

"Then do ten," I admonished. Jeez, did he not know there was a baby on board?

Kyle rolled his eyes, looked at me, and said, "It's going to be a long twelve days."

16

KEEPING SECRETS

Twelve. Days.

Has there ever been a longer period of time? God made the heavens and the earth in less than a week. Waiting to hear about our baby would take 288 hours. That's 17,280 minutes, or more than a *million* seconds. It was an impossible amount of time.

After arriving home from a ride during which all I did was frantically tell Kyle to slow down every other minute, I shuffled to the couch like an old woman, where I spent the next four days. I had been advised to spend two days resting, and I decided that if two days were good, four days were better. When I did have to move around the house to pee or eat the most nutritious superfoods I could find, I shuffled like an Egyptian mummy from an old horror movie. Every little cramp led to a spike of excitement mixed with panic. I was in a constant state of vigilance about my body, and while I tried not to think negatively, after all we had been through, it was hard to avoid. I worried that my worry would cause problems with my body, which caused me to worry more. If all this led to yet another failed test, I was certain I would shatter into millions of sharp shards and never be able to be repaired.

On day seven we had to fly to Chicago, where Kyle had media obligations ahead of NASCAR's season-ending Chase for the playoffs. I called Mary at REACH at least twenty times to ensure that the altitude and pressure changes during the flight and the speed and landing and everything else that comes with flying were safe for the baby. Surprisingly, she never changed her phone number and on every single call she assured me that yes, it was all very safe. And so, with white-knuckled terror, I boarded the flight.

As soon as we checked into the hotel, I hopped on my phone looking for the nearest drugstore.

"What are you doing?" Kyle asked. "Do you need something?"

"I can't take it anymore. I'm buying a pregnancy test and taking it first thing tomorrow morning."

"Babe, they told us we could get false negatives this early." He looked at me with obvious concern in his eyes. "I'm not sure it's such a good idea."

As he was talking, I found a nearby Walgreens and ran out the door.

"I know," I yelled over my shoulder as the door was closing, "but I have to check!"

The next morning, we bounded out of bed together and into the bathroom. I tore the package open and tossed the cardboard on the floor. I knew how to pee on a stick by this point, but we crammed into the bathroom together and checked and double-checked to make sure I was doing it right. Once again, we found ourselves sitting together on a bathroom floor, overwhelmed by emotion as the seconds ticked by. We held hands and prayed, whispering our most desperate wishes to God. Please, please let us be pregnant. Soon, I could see the beginning of a second pink line forming next to the one printed on the stick.

"What does a second line mean?" Kyle was scrambling through the torn-up cardboard packaging on the floor for the instructions.

"Pregnant," I whispered. Then louder, excited, I squealed, "It means we're pregnant!"

Pregnant! The word swirled around in my mind, shining light in every dark corner like the brightest dawn. We kissed, and cried, and kissed some more, lying there on the hotel bathroom floor in the city where we were married, completing a circle that seemed almost destiny. I started to call my mom, but when she answered in a voice thick with sleep and concern, I was overcome with emotion and couldn't speak. Gently, Kyle took the phone from my shaking hands to tell her the good news. Through the speaker, I could hear her excited cheering and crying. Finally, Kyle held the phone to my ear, and I found my voice.

"Mom," I squeaked through tears, "we finally did it."

She told me how much she loved me and showered me with congratulations before hanging up to tell my dad. When Kyle hung up the phone, I realized I was already rubbing my belly with my left hand, comforting the child who was already taking form inside me. Kyle lifted me out of the bathroom and gently laid me on the bed. He raised my shirt and kissed my belly over and over and started talking to our son.

"Hello, Son," he said. "You grow big and strong in there. I love you. I love you so much. I'll always be here for you." I never believed I could feel as full of joy and love and pride as I did in that moment. We had tried for so long that I wanted to shout from the rooftops. Instead, I called Mary at REACH, who cautioned me that it was still early in the pregnancy, and to be safe they would still want to run three series of blood tests. This was the standard protocol, and given the difficulty we had in getting pregnant, I understood. But it couldn't bring me down. My heart was so full of joy, so certain of our child. Period. End of story.

Kyle had to leave for his media obligations, and he kissed me goodbye, leaving me to enjoy Chicago on my own for the day. But before he left, he suggested we keep our news quiet aside from telling our parents, just in case things didn't work out the way we wanted them to. After showering, I got dressed and went out to find some breakfast. As I exited, the doorman swept the hotel's double doors wide open for me with a smile. "Oh, how sweet of you," I said as I skipped out the door, "holding the door for a pregnant woman!"

Walking the streets of Chicago, I thought about how the best days of my life had happened in this city. I remembered walking these streets with my grandmother and wished she were here to share in the news I wasn't sharing with anyone at all. Nope. Nobody.

I popped into Zara, and soon I had half of the baby section at the checkout counter. "I'm pregnant," I told the clerk, as I held up the cutest little pair of baby sneakers you've ever seen, "and these are for our son."

"Wow," she exclaimed, "look at you. I couldn't even tell. How far along are you?"

"Fourteen days," I beamed.

"Do you mean fourteen weeks?" she asked, confused. "Nope, fourteen days!" I decided to grab a cab back to the hotel instead of walking with all my baby gear. As I got into the cab, I immediately told the driver to be careful, there was a pregnant lady on board. Yep, I knew how to keep a secret all right.

Later that night, we had a NASCAR cocktail reception to celebrate the season and the upcoming Chase. Several times, Kyle had to gently remove my hand from its new home on my belly. I sidled up the bar and, in a conspiratorial whisper, told the bartender I was pregnant, but we weren't telling anyone and asked him to make a mocktail. A few minutes later, a server walked by offering a tray of sushi.

"I can't," I said. "I'm pregnant. Don't tell anyone. It's a secret!"

17

PREGNANCY— IS THIS NORMAL?

Like a mist creeping in over a storm-driven ocean, my morning sickness arrived. It began as an early aversion to foods I used to love: apples, sweet potatoes, and even the mere thought of meat would cause my stomach to slowly roll on the waves, right up to the edge of capsizing; then smells joined the group—a raspberry-vanilla air freshener caused my nose to wrinkle in disgust, and being near anyone with heavy cologne or perfume became torturous.

As my pregnancy continued, though, so did my progesterone injections, and before long morning sickness became morning, noon, and night sickness. The roiling ocean was now a raging tsunami, carrying me to dizzying heights and crashing me down into dark, deep troughs. I was always nauseated and could find no respite at all. I spent most of my days on the couch wrapped in a cozy blanket, cuddling with our dog, Lucy. Always present on the coffee table were untouched saltines and ginger ale, yet even these would send my stomach lurching.

On one such morning, I shot up out of bed from a deep sleep knowing I was seconds away from throwing up. I moved as fast as I could down the hallway to our bathroom, hoping I would somehow make it in time. But that hope was not to be, and I vomited all over the floor. Now, I know this is a common thing—many women with morning sickness have accidents like this—but what nobody tells you is that when you wake up you really have to pee. So, there I found myself with soaked pants in the middle of a puddle of my own vomit in the hallway, thinking that this was not at all what I thought pregnancy would be like.

Of course, even when you are sick, life continues. Most important, I still had to go to REACH for my many appointments. There were blood draws and ultrasounds and examinations to make sure all was well with our baby. The clinic was an hour away, and early morning appointments meant even earlier wakeups.

For one of these visits, I woke up at 6:00 AM, even more nauseated than usual. Kyle was out of town for an appearance, and I didn't want to bother anyone else for a drive as it was so early in the day, so I decided to go it alone. I managed to pull on a pair of jeans and some gym shoes, and toss my hair up into something that looked less rat's nest and more "don't mess with me, I'm pregnant," all the while certain that I was about to lose whatever was somehow still in my stomach. Nevertheless, I eased my way into the car; took a few slow, deep breaths that did nothing to stop the churning in my gut; and started the engine. I took my trusty puke bucket and placed her on the seat next to me. Yes, it was a she. Do you think I'd pour my guts out to any strange man?

I held it together as I rolled down our road, continuing the slow breathing and focusing on just making it there. After a few minutes I turned out of our neighborhood, and a volcano of nausea erupted in my stomach, accompanied by an intense dizziness. Suddenly, there was a loud banging on my car that snapped me to attention, and I realized with horror that I had veered off the road into a flock of geese. Looking outside my driver's window, I saw blood smearing the glass in thick, red stripes. This triggered a round of dry heaving, and I sat helpless in the driver's seat as geese surrounded my car, squawking loudly and glaring at me with their beady black eyes.

After a minute of panic, afraid to get out and check the damage—those birds were *mad*—I realized there was nothing I could do about the situation right then. I couldn't save the geese, and hitting a bird didn't seem like the kind of thing you call the police about. The dizziness had passed—maybe the adrenaline of the situation knocked it out for a bit—and I decided to push on.

Along the way, people honked and waved and tried to get my attention. My driver's side mirror had broken in the incident, and it dangled from a couple of wires thumping loudly against my door as I drove, and I thought maybe that's what they were trying to tell me. Based on some of the horrified stares, however, I also knew that the carnage spread across the outside of my car was probably bad, and they were right.

Now remember, at this point, apples—the least offensive food on the planet—made me sick. So, when I arrived at the clinic and got out of the car, you can imagine what happened. Before opening the door, I was already shaking and dry heaving and fighting back tears in anticipation of what was to come. I stepped out of the car, and the broken mirror clanged loudly against the door. Beneath the blood on the window was even more carnage, and you don't even want to know what was stuck in my grille.

I lurched forward, hands on knees, my stomach trying to force itself empty, but there was nothing to vomit. I heaved, and I cried, and I heaved some more, unable to get it together enough even to stand up. At this time, REACH was undergoing some renovations, and one of the construction workers saw my distress and my car and came over to help.

"Miss, are you okay? What happened?" he asked with concern.

Through my tears and retching, I tried to explain. Not unkindly, he laughed, a smoke-cured sound that was warm and raspy all at once. He explained that he had five kids and thought he had seen it all with his wife's pregnancies—until now. He told me to go inside, and he and his crew would take care of it.

When I came back outside after my appointment, all the blood and viscera and feathers were gone from my car. The mirror was duct-taped into place, and the grille was as put together as it could possibly have been given the circumstances. I will always be grateful to that construction crew; that day they truly saved me from driving home in a car that looked like a crime scene.

It was this all-day sickness that drove our decision to announce our pregnancy at nine weeks. This is far earlier than most people share their news, but one weekend at the Kansas racetrack, I had a harder time than usual keeping down anything at all. Even water would come right back up, and the mere thought of food had me running to the bathroom where the smooth porcelain of the toilet rim and I were becoming fast friends.

After two whole days of not being able to keep anything at all down, Kyle came in from practice to find me there, curled on the tile in front of the toilet, wrapped with my blanket, and cuddled with Lucy. He told me I looked ashen, and that he was worried about me and the baby. He wanted me to go to the infield care center, where drivers and NASCAR personnel received medical care during race weekends. Feeling too sick to reply, I simply held my arms up in agreement, and he scooped me off the floor. With a quick kiss on his way back to practice, Kyle loaded me into the golf cart with our motorhome driver, Kerby, and we were on our way.

When we entered, I called the doctor aside and in whispered tones told him I was pregnant and that we were not telling anyone yet. I was so quiet because there may have been members of the media or other drivers or industry pros in the area also receiving treatment, and I did not want our news getting out yet. He nodded his understanding, and the medical team quickly got to work running tests. They confirmed I was dehydrated but was not otherwise sick. The doctor also checked the baby's heartbeat and announced loudly enough to be heard over the roaring engines at the track that the baby was fine too and that I just had bad morning sickness.

The look I shot him must have conveyed what I was thinking, because he immediately lowered his voice to the lowest audible level to tell me they would be rehydrating me and keeping an eye on me for a little while. After two bags of IV fluids, I started feeling better and was soon on my way back to my blanket fort—which I was able to relocate from the bathroom to the couch.

But the next day, gossip was spreading through the drivers' motorhome area that I might be pregnant. Well, I hadn't gone through hell and back to allow anyone else to announce our pregnancy. So, the Monday after race weekend, Kyle and I met with a photographer with a perfect plan in mind to announce our pregnancy. We are a car family, so with my pink 1960s T-Bird, Kyle's 1956 teal Chevy Bel Air, and a vintage pedal car restored by Kyle's dad, Tom, we set our plan in motion. We parked all three cars in the middle of a beautiful grassy pasture flooded with evening sunlight and colorful bursts of wildflowers. Kyle and I held hands and breathed in the enormity of what we were about to do. Telling the world made it feel even more real. Dressed in our 1950s best, we were photographed with a sign that read, "Baby Busch racing at you, May 2015," and we announced our pregnancy.

Our baby continued to grow healthily, and at ten weeks I was able to come off the progesterone shots—and boy, was my butt happy about this. After so many weeks and so many shots, it was perpetually bruised and sore; a butt can only take so much. Over the next few weeks, the fog of the all-day sickness began to recede like it arrived, slowly over a calming sea. Soon, the sun broke through and my spirits and energy rose. I was even able to start leaving the house without my trusty puke bucket by my side!

As the sickness left and I was able to eat more than antinausea meds on a regular basis, another pregnancy truism arrived: cravings! Right around Thanksgiving, when I was three months pregnant, I spent two weeks putting cocktail sauce on *everything*—eggs, chicken, celery sticks, crackers, it didn't matter. Then one night at about midnight, I was going to *die* if I did not get a Taco Bell bean burrito in my face, and I had never in my life even eaten a bean burrito. I had no idea what it even tasted like, but it didn't matter. I needed it, and I needed it right then.

So Kyle and I loaded into the car and started a burrito quest. He was so excited. "Finally, a craving that works for me too!" The first Taco Bell we found was closed, and I was crushed. The second was also closed, and I was getting desperate. Every closed store magnified my craving until it became an obsession. Finally, after an hour of middle-of-the-night searching, we found an open Taco Bell and loaded up: two bean burritos, nachos, tacos, slushies—the works. I could feel myself salivating as the salty, cheesy, beany scents filled the car. Before Kyle even left the window, I was tearing off the paper wrapping of this manna from the gods and took a big bite, waiting for the explosion of flavors to satisfy my craving.

Boy, was I wrong. Mid-chew and mouth wide open, I realized this was not heaven sent, but it was the most disgusting thing I had ever put in my mouth. I *hated* bean burritos. Now I remembered why in almost thirty years of life I had never before ordered one. With that craving thoroughly shut down, I turned to Kyle and said sweetly, "Did I say bean burrito? I meant McDonald's chicken nuggets." Kyle, the dark circles under his eyes more pronounced than ever, simply said, "No." I spit out the burrito, we drove home, and I raided the pantry for items to douse in cocktail sauce. That was the first and the last of our late-night food quests.

The weirdest of my cravings, though, was not for food but for ice-cold water straight from a garden hose. Yep, hose water. No spring water, no tap water. No fancy water in a glass bottle or with bubbles in it. It had to be from a garden hose. These cravings always came at night, and they were always fierce. They were an itch that was right in the spot of your back that no amount of twisting and turning can reach and are the only thing you can think about. Kyle laughed it off at first, but as the intensity of my cravings grew, he realized he was going to have to do something about it.

Luckily, there are water hookups for motorhomes at all the NASCAR racetracks, and we were hooked up through—you guessed it—a hose. Thinking quickly, Kyle ran outside, disconnected the hose, and filled up a big glass for me. I saw the condensation running down the outside of the glass in big, fat beads when he came in, and I gulped it down. It was icy cold, and the most delicious thing I had ever tasted. I felt like I had been crawling in a desert and had just stumbled on the lushest, greenest oasis. I drank two more glasses, sediments and all, before I was finally sated.

The next day I called Barb, my midwife, as I had been transferred out of REACH's care and to a regular OB-GYN clinic at this point in my pregnancy, to ask her about it. Barb is amazing. She is kind, and smart, and listens. And really, really cares. She is everything I wanted an OB-GYN to be. She told me my body probably needed some mineral I used to get out of hose water as a kid. The brain is a funny thing, especially when pregnant.

So are our bodies. Weird pregnancy things seem to come one after the other, and when the cravings ended, something else started. I noticed I had a weird taste in my mouth, like the beginnings of bad breath, but it was always present. No amount of gum or mints or brushing would make it go away. Soon my tongue started to turn a fuzzy white. I went out and bought a tongue scraper, but it made no difference. I bought the strongest mouthwash, but a few minutes after spitting the lava-like liquid down my drain, my mouth would taste like July armpits again.

As I very cutely stood in front of the mirror one evening, scraping white gunk off my protruding tongue with a flat-bladed scraper, I noticed Kyle was staring at my back. "What?" I asked, trying to twist and see. Suddenly he poked me just beneath my right shoulder blade.

"Does that hurt?" If he had an Australian accent, he would have been just like the crocodile hunter, sneaking up on some wild animal and poking it to see what would happen.

"No," I exclaimed, annoyed. "Why, am I broken out again?

"No, no. It's just . . . well . . . you have these weird white freckles and blotches on your back. Like, *all over* your back." Alarmed and confused, I called Barb again. She had me come in and instantly told me I had a type of yeast infection *in my mouth and on my back*. I was so disgusted with my body.

She prescribed a rinse for my mouth that tasted a lot like a banana cream pudding I thoroughly enjoyed while having cravings. And for my back? Selsun Blue dandruff shampoo, slathered on my back every other day and then covered in plastic wrap for forty-five minutes. So, I wrapped myself up like the bean burrito I hated, swished banana pudding medicine in my mouth for a few weeks, and sure enough, everything went away. Good ol' Barb. She's like the *Encyclopedia Britannica* of pregnant-girl problems.

As weeks passed and my body settled down, I came to adore the swelling of my stomach. Kyle and I had so much fun documenting our weekly bump updates, and even took a special "babymoon" trip to Anguilla. We had fought so hard to get here, and now the magic was starting to sparkle through. Everything up until this point had been a struggle, and finally, *finally* we could start to enjoy it. We couldn't wait to become parents.

And that's when, on a February morning, Kyle wrecked at Daytona.

18

CRASHING DOWN

The SUV screeched to a halt at the front doors of the hospital emergency department. My heart was racing, it was getting hard to hold back the tears, and my breath was coming in short little gasps. I remember the hospital lobby was full of people waiting for care, some with bandages covering cuts and scrapes, others with ailments I couldn't detect just by looking at them. I told a kind woman at the reception desk that my husband had been in an accident at the racetrack.

"What's your husband's name, sweetie?" she asked, a sharp northern Florida twang in her voice.

"Kyle Busch," I replied, my voice hitching partway through.

She paled slightly and whisked me back to a more private waiting area, where the few of us who had been in the SUV could wait for news. "Sit here, honey," she said.

"No," I said. "I have to see him."

"They're evaluating him right now. Someone will be out to talk to you soon."

"But I have to see him," I wailed. It was all I could think about: Kyle alone on the other side of two large metal doors leading into the emergency department, in pain and maybe in danger, and there was no way for me to get to him. I wondered if he knew I was here, or if he was even conscious. I wondered if he was scared and upset that I wasn't there to face this with him. If I could have ripped those doors down with my bare hands, I would have.

A flood of people poured into the waiting area. The NASCAR chaplain arrived first, took my hand, and prayed with me. While his rich baritone was comforting, I couldn't focus on anything except getting into the emergency department to see Kyle. Soon, administrators from Kyle's race team, NASCAR executives, and other people from the sport came in to offer support and encouragement. Everyone meant well, but it was overwhelming to constantly be asked what I knew and how he was, and I excused myself to the bathroom for a moment of privacy. I couldn't understand why nobody had come out to talk to me yet, and my mind wandered to the worst.

On the way to the bathroom, I marched up to the security guard sitting outside the doors to the treatment area and demanded access. He kindly but firmly refused and said that if I would just stay in the waiting area, somebody would be out to talk to me just as soon as they had something to tell me. He'd clearly had this conversation before, but I hadn't, and in that moment, I hated him. I needed someone to blame, and he was it. I glared at him and stomped off to the bathroom. Once inside, I locked the door behind me and started to cry, the tears gushing out in long, racking sobs. Each inhale was a struggle, coming with a shudder against a throat that was so tight with emotion I didn't know if it would ever open again. I sat down on the floor, back against the wall and my knees tucked tight up against my chest.

There was a knock on the door.

"Samantha, open up, honey." My mother's voice, as familiar as my own face, floated into the room. I had totally forgotten she had been up in the stands with Pops at the race, and gratitude and relief flooded through me. They were exactly who I needed in that moment; their steady and reassuring presence and fierce love kept the last strands of my sanity from fraying. I opened the door and melted into her arms, crying into her shoulder while Mom stroked my hair and held me until I was cried out.

"Mom, nobody will tell me anything," I said when I was able to speak again. "I'm so scared."

She pulled back, hands on my shoulders, part holding me up, part holding me back from the edge. "Samantha, you will get through this. You're strong, *so* strong. And Kyle needs that from you. He needs you to be the strong one now. Your baby needs you to be strong right now. We're in it together, as a family, and you're the center of that family."

I looked her in the eye, seeing her belief in me, and drew strength from her. I nodded briefly, took a deep breath, and drew myself up to my full height. I felt the knot of panic in my chest begin to loosen, and in its place came a white-hot spark of anger. I wasn't going to be held back.

Mom saw this in me too, smiled, and said, "Good. Now let's go get some answers."

I marched back to the security guard and again demanded to see someone and get an update. He stonewalled, giving me his rote "Someone will be out soon" answer before looking away. A nurse opened the door and came out, and I grabbed her. She gave me the same line, that someone would be out "soon." That wasn't good enough, and I let her know it.

"Look at me," I pleaded. "I am *pregnant*. I need to see my husband, and I need to see him now. At least just tell me if he is alive!"

"Okay," she said. "Okay. You can go back. But *just* you," she said, gesturing at the assembled mass in the waiting room. I looked and realized it had turned into something of a circus. More family members and friends and NASCAR officials and team members had filled the small room to bursting, all of them with grim faces and worried eyes. I agreed, squeezed my mom's hands, and blowing past the security guard followed the nurse through the swinging metal doors.

I was in a long hallway filled with aggressive fluorescent lighting. The tile floor was somehow both dull and gleaming, a trick of its hard-to-stain beige coloring. There was nothing in the space to absorb sound, and my heels made a sharp, echoing *clack* with every step. It was like a horror movie. The hallway seemed to stretch out in front of me, each step taking me no closer to its end. I walked faster, needing more than anything to see Kyle, to hug him, to be there for him.

After what seemed an eternity, we turned a corner into a large bay. There was a central nursing station and several treatment areas separated by long curtains dangling from runners along the ceiling. They were all open and empty except one, outside of which two doctors were talking in low tones with urgent gestures. The nurse walked straight up to them, and I followed.

"This is Mrs. Busch," she said.

"How is he? What's going on? Is he alive?" I blurted, the words tumbling out of my mouth. Once they started talking, it was hard to get them to stop. All the sounds of the hospital seemed to disappear, and the doctors came into crystal-clear focus. I could hear their breathing, see the dark shadow of afternoon stubble on one of their cheeks. I could smell the hospital soap on their hands and see every minute stain on their bright white coats. One of them took a breath and started to speak.

In that moment, I flashed back to the minute before we learned that we were pregnant in the hotel room in Chicago. I remembered the tile floor of the bathroom where we sat, waiting for a line to appear, the squares so different from this hard, flat, industrial flooring on which I now stood. In each place we were teetering on a precipice, an overwhelming surge of emotion that could elevate us to the highest peaks or catapult us into the depths of despair. This microsecond filled the entirety of history and a chaos of possible futures would close off depending on what he said.

"He's very seriously injured," the doctor said.

I started to tumble into the void.

"But it's not life-threatening. He's going to survive."

Relief rushed into my body, but there was more I needed to hear.

"We're trying to bring a specialist in to do his first surgery."

Wait. *First* surgery? And with that, I moved. I pulled back the curtain surrounding Kyle's bed, and there he was.

A nurse was using a long silver pair of shears to cut Kyle's fire suit off. She went down from his thigh, across his knee and down to his ankle, and the end of the shear's journey was his left foot, dangling off the end of the bed at an angle that made no sense for a foot. It was pointing away from Kyle's body and somehow backward at the same time, drooping lazily toward the floor. With horror, I started to look up to his face, my eyes floating across his right leg along the way, and there, jutting out of a red nightmare, was a white shard of bone.

I gasped and felt my vision start to go gray. No, I told myself. No, not now. I remembered my mother telling me that I needed to be the strong one, and I pulled it together. Kyle's face came into focus, lined with pain and worry. I ran up to the head of the bed and kissed him all over his face, my hot tears splashing down on him. Before I could say anything, he asked if the baby and I were okay. I couldn't believe it—his foot was literally dangling off the end of his leg, he was about to be rushed into emergency surgery, and he was asking *me* if I was okay? A rush of love for this man pushed away some of the intense fear.

"I don't think I'll be racing in the Daytona 500 tomorrow," he said grimly. I agreed, and my heart broke for him.

One of the doctors—the one with the five-o'clock shadow—gently touched my elbow and asked if he could speak to me outside. I kissed Kyle on the forehead and stepped a few feet away to the nursing station where the doctor and I could speak.

"Well, as you can see, he's broken both his tibia and his fibula in his right leg—these are the bones in his shin. He's also shattered his left foot.

It's really bad, and it's going to take a lot of work to repair it." He paused for a moment, giving me space to let this news sink in.

"Will he have permanent damage?" Thinking, *Please, God, don't let him lose the use of his leg or foot.*

"No, nothing like that," he reassured me, "but it will be a long and hard road to recovery. There's a specialist in tibia and fibula surgery about an hour away. What I'd recommend is having him come in and operate on his leg now. Then, when he's had a few days to recover, we can airlift him back to Charlotte for the foot surgery. We're already working with the NASCAR medical team there to make sure he'll have the absolute best care."

That's when the enormity of everything hit me. Our lives were about to change dramatically, and we were so unprepared. There wouldn't be weekends at racetracks, waking up together in the motorhome we had built, no more joint workouts or long walks through the park with our dog, Lucy. We were ready for our lives to change just a few months away with the baby, but not now, not like this.

I agreed to the treatment plan, and a huge stack of papers to sign was placed in front of me. I think the nurse could sense just how overwhelmed I was, because even though she had insisted I was the only person allowed back here, a few minutes later she appeared with my mom in tow. Together, while Kyle was wheeled away for more X-rays and scans and tests, we went through each sheet. By the time we were done, the specialist had arrived, and Kyle was returned to his space behind the curtain. We all joined him there.

The doctor introduced himself, his voice warm and strong in the cold, sterile room. I could sense his competence through the way he talked, an experienced mix of honesty and encouragement. "I've operated on many athletes," he said, "and while the road back will be tough, by August you should be good as new."

"That's six months away, Doc. That's not going to work," groaned Kyle from the bed.

"What do you mean?"

"I've got to be back in top form by mid-May. I've got to get back to racing, and my son will be born. There is no way in hell I'm watching my son's birth from a wheelchair."

The doctor looked at Kyle with puzzled eyes. "I really don't think that's possible. Your body is going to need time to heal, real time, and it's going to take a lot of therapy just to get you walking again, let alone racing. We'll get you there, but not by May."

"Sorry, Doc, but there's the All-Star race in May. I'll be using it as a practice run, and the next week, I'll be driving in the Coke 600. Mark my words." The Coke 600 is the longest race of the season. Of course.

"Well," he said, "we'll cross that bridge when we get there. I've just never seen it happen. But, first things first, let's get this leg taken care of." He excused himself to prep for surgery. Mom soon followed, and it was just the two of us. We held each other, and we prayed. I tried my best to keep a brave face, holding back the tears and doing everything I could to keep Kyle calm before the operation. I like to think I helped, but I'll bet the morphine also had something to do with it. Soon, several nurses appeared, ready to take Kyle off to surgery. I told him I loved him and that I'd be there when he woke up before kissing him goodbye.

Soon, a nurse came back to let me know Kyle was in surgery and to escort me to a new waiting area. Larger than the last, it was still overflowing with people there to support Kyle. Through the windows, I could see fans and media members and others just waiting to hear news of how he was doing. I couldn't believe the outpouring of love and concern and was full of gratitude.

That's when I noticed I hadn't felt the baby kick in hours.

I froze right there in the doorway, a sudden icy-cold panic worming its way back into my heart. Our son was normally so active, flipping and flopping around in my womb. His fluttering was my constant companion, an ever-present reminder that he was there, and he was safe. Except now he wasn't. I grabbed the nurse and told her I hadn't felt him kick in a long time.

"It's okay," she said. "He probably just senses that you're worried. Try to stay calm, not to worry, and you'll feel him soon."

Don't worry? That's easy for her to say. I was six months pregnant; my husband's bones were sticking outside his leg; we'd just had a completely uncertain future thrust upon us in the blink of an eye. "I'm really scared," I whispered.

She glanced around the room, took my arm, and walked me back through the double doors. "You're not a patient here, so don't tell anyone I did this. I could get in trouble." We rushed back to the space Kyle had been in, and after telling me to wait there she pulled the curtain and disappeared. A few minutes later, I heard her tell the nurse manning the station that she didn't see anything, and then she was back in the room carrying a small Doppler ultrasound attached to a speaker. "I haven't done this since nursing school, but let's see what we can find."

At first, there was nothing. No sound at all. She checked to make sure the speaker was on and the volume turned up, and then tried again. Still nothing. I began to sweat, the icy spike of panic blooming into a glacier of dread, and then I heard it, the high-pitched, steady gallop of my son's heartbeat. It was clear, and strong, and it filled the room like sunshine. I hugged the nurse, managed my first real smile in hours, and got cleaned up. We went back down the long hall, and she left me in the packed waiting room.

Kyle's surgery took several hours, and I tried to remain stoic, accepting the well wishes of everyone who had come to see us. Of course, I was just white-knuckling it on the inside. When someone you love is in surgery, every second is agony, and there were so many seconds. I felt the hard chair digging into my back and knotting my muscles. I stretched as best I could in the seat and watched the clock. Finally, when I could no longer take it, the doctor came out and whisked me to a small private room. Everything had gone fine, he assured me, and I would be able to see Kyle soon. I took a deep breath, letting some of the tension drain from my body.

The surgeon took me back to the recovery area, where I saw Kyle fast asleep. He looked so small and so vulnerable that it lit a fire inside me. He had always been the rock, the protector in our relationship, but now it was my turn. I sat down next to his bed, took out my phone, and started firing off emails. I emailed contractors to get the ball rolling on making our house wheelchair accessible. We needed ramps and railings and equipment. I called the insurance company and made sure they were going to cover all of the necessary medical gear and equipment. We'd need a hospital bed and a wheelchair van, and I got started on making that happen. I emailed members of Kyle's team to update them. I handled things because they needed to be handled. It was something I could do in a time when everything else was out of my control.

Beside me, Kyle began to stir. I put my phone away and stroked his hair until I saw his eyes open. There was pain in them, but I could also see he was there, alert. I made sure he knew I was there, told him the surgery was over, and that he was well, and I waited for him to come all the way to. As he did, the doctor returned.

"Your surgery went perfectly," he said, and gave us a technical explanation of the repair he did. It boiled down to us spending three days in the hospital in Daytona before being airlifted to Charlotte. It was the best news we could have expected, and we thanked him. Soon, Kyle was asleep again, and I sat vigil over his dreams. Around three o'clock in the morning, my dad came into the room and gently told me to go back to the motorhome and get some rest. "You'll need your strength, Samantha. I'll stay here and keep guard over Kyle." He was right, and so I did. Mom drove me to the motorhome and, exhausted, I let myself inside. As I undressed for bed, I saw Kyle's sweatshirt hanging over the back of a chair and put it on. I got into bed, bathed in his scent, and went to sleep with my arms wrapped protectively around our son.

19

ROAD TO RECOVERY

Afchen a short, fitful sleep, I returned to the hospital early the next morning. Everyone talks about the smell of hospitals, and it was no different here. Strong disinfectant chemicals overpowered the subtle floral scents drifting from an arrangement on the nurses' station. I checked in and was given a white sticker with VISITOR stamped on it in blue, and I stuck it on my chest. I was anxious, not quite sure what to expect from Kyle today. Would he be awake? In pain? How badly would his injuries turn out to be over time? The night and day before had been fueled by adrenaline, the immediacy of the emergency pushing me forward. It was a sprint; today was the first mile of a marathon.

Taking a deep, calming breath in through my mouth, I centered myself and walked into his room. My dad was still there, dozing in a blue recliner as Kyle slept next to him. Kyle's leg was in traction, raised high off the bed and wrapped in a bright white cast. His injured foot was covered under a blanket, but I could see the bulk of the bandages wrapped around it bulging under the cover. Tubes and wires snaked from his arm and chest, and a monitor silently traced his breathing, oxygen levels, and heart rate. His mouth was slightly open, his head deep in the uncomfortable hospital pillows, and his hair mussed. He looked so small, and so hurt, and I let out a small sob.

My dad heard this and stirred, pushing himself groggily forward in the uncomfortable chair. He winced as he stood, coming forward to hug me. I felt the bristle of his facial hair brushing against my cheek, and his strong arms wrapped around me like I was a child again. He held me as he explained that Kyle had slept straight through, and he'd probably be pretty medicated and sleepy all day. Pops then said he was going to go back and get some real sleep, rubbing his lower back after releasing me.

I took his place in the chair after wheeling it over closer to Kyle's bed. I took his hand, careful not to touch any of the wires or tubes. He didn't move, and I was left there to wonder what was next. It turns out it was nothing, more nothing, and then a lot more nothing. The waiting and watching was such a stark contrast to the nonstop action we would have been experiencing at the racetrack. After I spent an hour there, wandering in my own thoughts, a nurse walked in, introduced herself, and checked on Kyle. She told me the doctors were pleased with how Kyle was doing as she checked the readings on the equipment, and they thought he would probably sleep most of the day.

Soon, I heard a familiar buzzing whine, and it took me a minute to figure out what it was because it didn't belong here in the hospital. Finally, I realized we were close enough to the speedway that what I heard were the racecars screaming around the track. It struck a pang of sadness in my heart, and I wondered when I'd hear that sound again, but it was this sound that brought Kyle to. I felt him squeeze my hand, and his eyes opened slightly. He mumbled something that I couldn't hear, and I told him I was there and asked him to say it again.

"I should be there," he said, and there was such pain in his voice I almost started to cry. I promised him he'd be back and sooner than anyone thought. I promised him we would do it together. He nodded, eyes tight with pain, and settled back into the pillow. He asked me to turn on the TV, and we sat and watched the race from his room, silently holding hands. From time to time, a nurse would come in and give him some medicine or chart his vitals, but we were mostly left alone with each other. As soon as the race was over, Kyle fell back into a deep, medicated sleep. I kissed him on his forehead and made up the couch in the small attached room to get some desperately needed sleep of my own. As I fell back onto the hard, vinyl-covered cushions, gently holding my growing belly, I prayed for Kyle and our son. Everything felt raw, unfair, and surreal, and my eyes started to burn as tears built behind my lids. I squeezed my eyes shut and willed the tears to go away. I was determined to be the fighter my boys needed me to be.

That became our routine for the next couple of days. Kyle would mostly sleep and rest between doctors coming to check in while I sat next to him and furiously planned for the next phase of our life. I made sure that the contractors were hard at work at home and became the bane of our insurance company's existence. Strangely, I think throwing myself into this work kept me from facing the enormity of it. The details were the trees that kept me from seeing the forest. This insulation let me cope; it helped ease into the enormity of what we were facing piece by piece instead of taking it all on at once. I did my best to follow Nurse Mary's IVF mantra of "one step at a time" in this situation too.

The night before Kyle was to be airlifted back to Charlotte for his foot surgery, I was in the motorhome getting things packed up. We had learned that day that Lucy wouldn't be allowed on the medical plane, so my parents were going to drive back to Charlotte with her. After they packed up the car to return home, Mom came and held me as I worked to hold it together. "Everything's going to be okay," she assured me. "You can do this. You *are* doing it, and we will be here for you guys every step of the way." Then she turned to load her last bag into the trunk as Pops came to kiss me goodbye. "You've got a strong man in there, Samantha, and you need to hang in there for him and for the baby. I know you can do it." I went back into the motorhome and noticed that Lucy was still there in her carrier! Frantic, I turned to catch them before they left and saw my mom standing inside the door.

I lost it. Tears fell heavily off my cheeks and into Lucy's soft fur as I took her from her carrier. Shaking, I hugged her and sobbed. I'd already lost Kyle as my constant companion, and now Lucy was going, too. I felt as lonely as I'd ever been. I rocked with Lucy on the floor, while my mom sat next to me and rocked right along. "Mom, I'm so scared. Kyle's hurt so badly, and I have no clue what our life will be like with a new baby if he doesn't recover. I don't know how to do it." She stayed there supporting me in the way only a mother can until I was finally cried out. I gave Lucy one final squeeze and handed her to my mom. I watched until the taillights of their car were beyond the range of my sight.

The next morning, Kyle was wheeled into an ambulance for the trip to the airport. I rode along in the back with him. Kyle, who had been given extra pain meds for the journey, was joking that being able to avoid traffic was a big plus to breaking his bones when the lights and sirens started. After another short ride, we were being bundled into the plane. It was like a private hospital room inside, with the same monitors and tubes and machines filling the passenger area as Kyle had in his room. Our flight doctor and nurse introduced themselves, I strapped into a small chair where I could see Kyle without being in the nurse's way, and soon we were lifting into the air.

Beneath us, the track within the speedway traced a serpentine path, almost like a small river around the middle of the speedway. The sight of the track brought me back to the moment I heard Tony's voice calling out to Kyle over the radio, asking if he was okay, and a sudden flood of adrenaline brought back the terror of that moment. I started to sweat, my breath came quickly, and I grabbed the armrest of my chair in the flush of panic. Then we were in the clouds, Daytona disappeared, and the fear receded. I needed to be in the moment, not in the past. Despite the promises I'd made to Kyle, I wondered if we'd be back next year. Heck, I wondered if we'd be back at all. I believed in Kyle, but I couldn't stop seeing the bones sticking out of his right leg, and his other foot dangling at that crazy angle. Fear sat heavily in my stomach, and I didn't know if I *wanted* him back on the track.

It was a short flight to Charlotte, and soon we were in the back of another ambulance on the way to another hospital. We wheeled into Kyle's room, and it was a flurry of activity. His nurse for the day took the report from the flight nurse, who rattled off his injuries, the procedures that had been done, where every IV and other tube went, and all sorts of other information. I marveled that she was able to keep so much detail in her head. After two minutes of it, *my* head was swimming. As they talked, a team of nurses joined in with the flight crew to transfer Kyle from the stretcher onto his hospital bed. I was terrified they were going to drop him, but they did it without a hitch; a quick grimace from Kyle was the only indication that it hurt at all.

The next week was a dreary monotony punctuated by moments of anxiety around the surgical repair of Kyle's foot. I'll tell you what: hospitals are *exhausting* yet *boring* at the same time. You eat the same food every day and you sit and sleep in the same uncomfortable chair; the same staff come at the same time. People are constantly in and out of the room, whether medical staff, well-wishers, friends, or family, and I was the point person for all of them. I also had to make sure the medical upgrades to our house were on schedule and make sure Kyle's fans knew he was okay. The surgery went well, and after seven days in the hospital Kyle was discharged. Finally, we were going home.

We arrived home to find wheelchair ramps were set up to get in and out of the house. Dog gates were removed and tucked away to give us unfettered access. Our living room was converted into a hospital room, dominated by a large hospital bed. I had our mattress moved downstairs too, so I could be with Kyle while he slept, ready to lend a hand whenever he needed it in the middle of the night. Railings were put up in our bathroom to make it easier for Kyle to get in and out of his wheelchair in there, and if I'm being honest, I liked to use these over the weeks as my belly grew and grew. I almost didn't recognize the place.

The grin on Kyle's face when he got in the door of our home melted my heart. It was good to be back in our own place, with our own food and space and *quiet*. No one tells you that in hospitals you are constantly woken up by nursing checks, the sounds and visitors of other patients, alarms, and so on—not to mention that sleeping balled up in a chair isn't exactly comfortable, especially with a rather round belly. We hadn't had a good night's sleep in what felt like forever, but first, we were starving.

In the next few weeks, we would have been headed to the West Coast for the races. While he was crushed not to be driving, I think it was even worse for him that he wouldn't be able to get his favorite meal: In-N-Out Burger. So, I made a special copycat meal to celebrate being home. We ate together, Kyle sitting up in his wheelchair, lower than the other seats at the kitchen table. He looked like a little boy, and I jokingly offered to cut his hamburger for him. Across the table our eyes locked, and we laughed loudly together for the first time in a very long time. Things were going to be okay.

It wasn't easy, though—none of it was easy. That night, we both caught a whiff of each other. Yep, we needed a shower, a *real* shower, not a hospital wipe down, and then we realized we weren't sure how to make that work. I knew we couldn't get his casts wet, so I grabbed garbage bags and duct tape to wrap his leg and foot in, making him look like a mummy. We wheeled him into the bathroom but quickly realized there wasn't enough room to get his chair in the shower door, where we could transfer him to the special shower bench we had installed. I was going to have to support his weight for the few feet between the door and the bench.

At this point I was twenty-nine weeks pregnant, and I'm a pretty small person to begin with. Kyle put his weight on me, and I nearly collapsed. He shot his arms out to grab the shower door frame and bear some of the burden, but it was a real struggle to get him there. We twisted and turned to get through the doorway, and I practically flung him onto the bench. We took a minute to catch our breath, and then I started to gather the things he would need to clean himself up and even shave. This moment, Kyle admitting he needed my help and actually taking it, was huge. It was so hard for both of us, one of the touchstones in a marriage where each partner had to be completely vulnerable and open. We got through it, and I started gently shaving his face.

After that was done, we remembered we'd have to get him back to his wheelchair. Except now we were wet and slippery. I'm honestly not sure how we both didn't end up back in the hospital with broken bones, but somehow we managed it. I wheeled him back to bed, we got him transferred, and soon we'd both passed out from exhaustion.

As the days and weeks went on, we got better at navigating our new normal. Doctors, therapists, and specialists were constantly in and out of the house. It was humbling for Kyle, who is so fiercely independent and used to doing everything for himself. Now he wasn't able to do even many basic things, needing to rely on me to clip his toenails and take care of his wounds and healing routines. He struggled through it, learning how to ask for help and being okay with it. We both learned to not take each other or any of the small things for granted. Our fast-paced life slowed way, way down, and it strengthened our relationship. Together, we carefully set up the baby's nursery. We spent nights across our table playing cards like we did when we were dating. Some days, we tucked in together in Kyle's hospital bed, browsing online stores for baby clothes and discussing hopes and dreams for our son.

One evening, we were relaxing in the living room. I was reading a book on pregnancy while Kyle watched old races on our TV from his bed. We had been trying to pick out a baby name that was unique and fun, and every once in a while, one of us would toss a name out to the other. None of them stuck. The chapter I was reading in my pregnancy book was talking about Braxton-Hicks contractions—early, harmless contractions women experience during their pregnancies. I hadn't had any and wondered what they would feel like, and then it hit me.

"Babe," I started, my voice carrying the excitement I felt, "what about Braxton?"

He thought for a minute. "Hmm, that's not bad. What if we changed a vowel? Broxton? Brexton?"

"Yes!" I screamed, "Brexton!"

He thought some more and with a big grin said, "I love it!" It was unique and edgy and tough. Brex, B-Rex, T-Rex, so many nickname possibilities, and all of them great. It was the perfect name for the tough, wild, strong-willed little boy we imagined he would be. We had a name! *Brexton*. I said it over and over again in my mind, rubbing my belly and feeling more connected than ever before to the baby growing inside it.

Kyle had a goal, and he never wavered from it: he was going to walk into the hospital with me when our son was born. He made remarkable progress, although it still felt slow to him. His strength amazed me, and his progress stunned his doctors. The milestones we hit along the way during our pregnancy inspired him to work even harder. When we first found out I was pregnant, we made an appointment for our special thirty-three-week 3-D ultrasound and circled the date with eager antici-pation. We were so excited that we would get to see our son's face. I day-dreamed of his cute button nose, his chubby cheeks underneath closed eyes with long lashes. When the day came, Kyle wheeled in with me to the homey office, decorated with large pictures on the walls depicting sepia-toned images of sweet babies in utero. Some showed babies with the poutiest lips, others were sucking their thumbs, each one looked like a sleeping angel. I couldn't contain my excitement.

I found myself on a soft table in an exam room. A tech squirted a warm gel on my belly and moved the probe over it. I felt Kyle take my hand and squeeze it tightly. I squeezed back, and the two of us grinned at the screen as its golden glow bathed the room. "Hmm," said the sonographer, "he seems a little balled up in there. Come on, kiddo, show us your face!" Brexton didn't listen and continued to hide from us.

"Not to worry," she said. "I've got just the thing!" She picked up a glass jar from a nearby cart, half full of an assortment of coins. She stepped back to her station and put the gelled probe back on my belly, which was beginning to chill in the cool room. As Brexton's hands came into focus, she took the jar and rattled it loudly near my stomach. No dice: Brexton stayed just as he was. "Maybe try rolling on your side," she suggested, and I levered myself up and rolled to my right, facing the screen directly, where Brexton was exactly as he had been before, curled up tightly and hiding his face.

"Well, do you do yoga?" she asked. I told her I did, and she suggested I try Downward Facing Dog. Feeling absolutely ridiculous, I got down on my hands and knees, with my butt pointing up in the air and my belly swaying below me. She continued to move the probe around as I took deep breaths, craning my neck to see the screen. He hadn't moved at all.

"I'm so sorry," she said. "It looks like we're not going to get to see his face today." My heart fell. I was so looking forward to seeing my son. "But we did learn something important," she said, a bright sparkle of mischief in her voice.

"What did we learn?" Kyle asked. "I didn't see anything!"

"Well," she replied, "we learned that he's quite the headstrong little baby."

Kyle and I locked eyes and cracked up. "I don't know *where* he gets that," I said. Even though we didn't see his face, seeing this little flash of his personality—sharing a trait that Kyle and I both have in spades—made him feel like such a part of the family already.

Nevertheless, we loved the parts we did see. On the drive home, we talked about seeing Brexton's perfect little fists in sharp, yellow detail on the screen, and how his adorable feet with tiny toes floated across the screen like a dream. We kept moving forward, Kyle improving and me growing day by day. Our new normal began to feel less new and more normal, and we faced it together.

20

CALLED TO MAKE A DIFFERENCE

As Kyle's recovery continued to progress, we were overwhelmed with the love and support from his fans. Every day, piles of cards and letters came to our race shop, wishing him well and cheering him on. Every night we'd sit together in the living room and open each one, feeling our spirits rise as total strangers poured out their hearts and offered kindness. This was as healing as any surgery, refreshing our faith in humanity and reminding us how amazing the NASCAR community really is.

Occasionally, one of the letters would mention that the person writing it was also struggling with infertility. I'd been blogging about my experiences and found that our story was one that so many other people were also living. Some talked about how hard it was financially, and one even said they'd had to give up on their dream of having a baby because they couldn't pay for the treatments. Just around this time, we'd had a visit to the REACH clinic for a checkup. As we were walking in, another couple was walking out, pale and crying. I heard the husband tell his wife as we passed them how sorry he was that he couldn't pay for their treatments. He looked defeated with his shoulders slumped beneath the weight of the world, and the two of them walked slowly and sadly to their car as I cried my way into the building.

From the start of this process, I had been keenly aware of how lucky Kyle and I were. While we were struggling with many of the same challenges other couples faced when confronting infertility, we were so blessed to not have to worry about the financial aspect of it. Even so, I was struck by just how expensive the process was, and I was heartbroken that something as mundane as money could keep people from becoming parents.

The Bible tells us that faith without works is dead. When we got home from our appointment that night, I sat Kyle down in the living room, held his hand, and told him we needed to live our faith and do something. I told him what the looks on that couple's faces meant to me. I told him some of the stories of insurance not covering treatments that readers of my blog had shared with me. I told him that when I prayed, I felt God fill my heart with peace and the knowledge that we had gone through all this for a reason. I told him that we had the ability to help people have babies, the miracles they so desperately wanted, but their financial realities stood in their way. We had the opportunity to possibly end some of the stigma that surrounds infertility and empower couples with the knowledge to make their journeys more manageable, and I shared how *lonely* the process of infertility felt, and that I needed to do something to make women going through it feel less alone. This was my calling.

Kyle looked me right in the eye, took my hand, and said, "You've had a lot of great ideas, babe. This one is the best. Let's do it." We already had a foundation, and we changed its mission and its name to focus specifically on these problems. We started planning that night, figuring out what we needed to learn about, who we needed to bring on board, and all of the details we needed to attend to in order to make things happen. That's when the Samantha and Kyle Busch Bundle of Joy Fund was born.

21

PUSHING FORWARD

The last two days before the delivery and most of the day itself were a nonstop war between anxiety and excitement, and they started back on the racetrack for the first time since Kyle wrecked and was so badly injured. That's right, two days before our baby was born, Kyle was back in his racecar hurtling at almost 200 miles per hour around the track, inches from other cars doing exactly the same thing as the day he'd wrecked. I think I used all my birthing breathing lessons just getting through that day.

It was the NASCAR All-Star Race in Charlotte, the first of two back-to-back weekends in our hometown. It really was the perfect time for Kyle to get back onto the track from a driving standpoint. It was a no-pressure race since no points would be awarded to the winner, just a trophy and bragging rights. If he started driving and his reconstructed leg and foot just couldn't take it, there was no harm done in calling it early and coming back another week, but it was terrifying for me.

Before the race, the drivers are introduced to the crowd. When I heard Kyle's name come over the loudspeakers, the announcer's rich voice echoed across the track to the loudest cheers I've ever heard, and panic set its cold teeth in my stomach. It was too soon for Kyle to be back racing. Heck, five years from now would be too soon. I was literally hours away from giving birth to his baby, and all I could see in my mind was him shooting out of control across the infield grass at Daytona, plowing straight into a concrete wall. But Kyle is a man of his word, and making it back so quickly after such a serious injury was a huge achievement, and the fans let him hear their admiration.

Just before the race started, we stood next to his car listening to the prerace prayer over the loudspeakers. For probably the millionth time that day, I poured my soul into it, asking God for safety for Kyle and our baby. Sensing my fear, Kyle grabbed me around the waist, pulling me into a deep kiss. With a reassuring smile, he told me to keep my legs crossed so the baby didn't fall out while he was driving, and slid into the car. Climbing the steep stairs into the pit box—no easy feat when you're as round and pregnant as I was—I found my seat and did, in fact, cross my legs, and my fingers, and toes, and anything else I could think of to cross that might help keep Kyle safe. The familiarity of the screaming engines roaring past became a lulling rhythm that helped settle me. By the end of the race, in which Kyle safely placed sixth, I was finally able to breathe again, so proud of all his hard work that led to this moment.

I wish we could say we did something grand and exciting with our last day together before Brexton was born, but we were both jittery with anticipation and needed to burn off our nervous energy. We worked out in the morning and then spent the day washing our cars. That's right, the day before my son was born, I was standing in the front yard in a bikini, bare belly protruding in front of me, scrubbing wheel rims with a toothbrush. I know how ridiculous it sounds, but it was just the kind of mindless activity we both needed to stay calm and centered and prepare for the arrival of our son.

We felt we knew everything and had prepared ourselves and our home as far as we could. We'd watched every video, read every book, learned every tip and trick, scrolled through every website. We had taken baby CPR courses, learned first aid, and more, but we also knew we were entering uncharted territory. We didn't know what adding a baby to the house would do to our relationship; we only knew that our lives as we knew them were about to change dramatically. We tried to go to bed early, and after an extra-long prayer, Kyle wrapped his arms around me and we fell into a deep sleep.

I got up a few minutes earlier than usual and spent them reading *Jesus Calling* by Sarah Young. It's my favorite devotional, and the reassuring words filled me with hope and a deep, spiritual calm. As I read, I absently rubbed my belly, conscious of the fact that, by the end of the day, it would look and feel very different. I thanked God for Brexton and even for the difficult journey to get him. I thanked Him for our marriage and prayed for Him to fill us with the knowledge of how to be wonderful parents. I asked Him to always give us patience and love and that, most important, we would teach our son about a relationship with God. I asked Him for blessings and safety for me and especially for Brexton. Soon, I heard Kyle stirring behind me, and we went about the business of getting ready for the day.

We'd already packed our hospital bag, and as Kyle was loading it into the car, I took a long, hot shower, watching the water bead and roll down my belly. I spoke to Brexton, telling him that he was going to meet us soon, and that things were going to look and sound a lot different, but not to be scared: His mommy and his daddy would be there the whole time, and we loved him, and we would always be there for him. I told him how excited we were to meet him and how he was about to enter into a world full of people who already loved him so much. I turned off the water and gently toweled off before dressing in some very comfy maternity clothes. We left the house hand in hand, knowing that the next time we returned it would be as a family of three.

We checked into the hospital at 8:00 AM sharp. Our midwife, Barbara, was there with a hug and an excited smile to welcome us. "Look at you, Kyle. Walking in as promised. Are you all so excited?" she asked.

I really, really was, but I was also scared. I had read all about labor and intellectually understood what to expect, but I didn't *know* what it felt like. For my entire pregnancy, I had planned to have a natural birth. Every other part of this journey had been outside my control. This was the one thing that was all the way in my control, and it was important to me to hold on to this bit of power over the situation. I had discussed this at length with Barb, with mothers who had been through it, and practiced all the breathing and relaxation techniques I could find, but I was still scared. I was afraid of the pain. I was afraid of not being able to do it, but mostly I was afraid of the unknown. Still, I was confident and resolved to do this my way.

The room was much nicer than I'd expected. Most hospital rooms are pretty sparse, without much in the way of comforts. While this had the always-present hospital bed and vinyl-covered chairs, it also had a nice couch, a calming and colorful painting on the wall, and more space than I'd thought we would have. There was a dresser with plenty of room for flowers, a large window that let sunlight stream in, and a vibrant energy. It was much homier and more comfortable than any hospital room I had ever been in, and I appreciated it so much. Barb handed me a light pink gown with darker pink decorative leaves on it and asked me to get changed. Kyle snapped the gown shut in back and then snapped some photos to send to our families.

Soon, a young nurse came in to start an IV in my right hand to deliver the Pitocin, the medication that would induce labor. Then, we waited. And waited. And waited. Several hours passed without much happening. Around noon, they came in to try to break my water, but I wasn't very dilated yet and the angle of the amniotic sac wasn't great, and it didn't work. Mom and Pops arrived, and there were hugs, well wishes, and an excited feeling in the room. Soon after, some close friends who worked nearby came to visit, and the hugging started up again. There was so much love in the room that I just knew everything was going to go perfectly.

Finally, around two in the afternoon, Barb was able to break my water. She used a long, shiny metal hook. There was a little tug, a small gush of warm liquid, and that's when labor really kicked in. At first, it wasn't too bad. The pain would build like the crescendo of an orchestra, reaching a high, chaotic peak and then decrescendo to a lower level. I started to feel hot and uncomfortable in the formerly soft and cool hospital gown, so I stripped down to a cream-colored bralette and mesh hospital underwear.

I was getting more and more uncomfortable. I tried to manage the contractions by sitting on a yoga ball, splitting my weight between the ball and my thighs. Soon though, the contractions became too strong for me to manage, and my legs gave out. I switched to bending over the ball, Kyle pushing down hard on my back and hips to try and give me some relief, but there was none to be had. The contractions were so powerful that I wasn't able to sway or breathe the way I'd been taught, and this started me into a spiral. I was panicking; the pain was growing beyond anything I could have imagined. I went on like this for hours, trying to stick to my plan. This was my one bit of control, I told myself, and tried to get my mind right.

After about three hours, I had only dilated to 7 centimeters. We needed to get to 10. I felt like my insides were being shredded, torn apart on a molecular level, until all that was left was pain. I didn't think I could take one more second of it. I was so angry at myself, feeling like a wimp and a failure, and I started crying. Kyle was rubbing my back in constant circles, and Barb took my hand and looked me straight in the eyes as if she were peering deep into my soul. I felt so connected to her, like she was right there in the trenches with me. It was a powerful moment, and I will always be grateful to her for sticking with me through it all.

Finally, Barb and Kyle together started talking to me about the epidural. They told me I wasn't any less of a woman for having it, and that it was more important that I was relaxed and happy and able to welcome Brexton into the world in a good state of mind than it was to stick to my plan. They were right. I tapped out and asked for the epidural.

Soon (although not nearly soon enough) an anesthesiologist was putting a monster of a needle into my spine. After the pain of the contractions, you'd think this was nothing, but it hurts like the devil himself is stabbing you with his own pitchfork. The flood of agony pulled back to a river, then a stream, then a trickle, and then it was gone. It's a strange experience losing the feeling in the lower half of your body, but it sure beats feeling like your guts are being lit on fire and their ashes are being stirred around with a poker.

Finally, I was able to relax. I talked with my family, and realized I was starving. I had been told not to eat all day because of the Pitocin, but that just wasn't going to happen anymore. I had Kyle sneak me some pretzels and I even wolfed down a protein bar. I felt a lot better after eating—they don't call it labor for nothing—and I had used up a lot of energy. After another hour or so, the nurse came in, checked my cervix, and said I had made it to 10 centimeters. It was time to push!

And I pushed. And pushed. And pushed some more, but nothing was happening. We all thought this part would go quickly since Brexton was supposed to be on the smaller side and I had been working out all during my pregnancy. But it was not to be. And suddenly, nausea rushed in. I'd give three big pushes, spit up into a bucket, suck in some oxygen from a plastic mask with a green elastic headband, and get ready to push some more. Barb asked me if I had eaten, and I sheepishly confessed that I had. She scolded me and let me know that's why I felt so bad. But we kept at it.

Barb gave me one end of a knotted sheet to pull on, thinking that might help. It didn't. Then she suggested a mirror so that I could see what was going on and watching the birth might help keep me motivated to push, as if I needed more motivation. But I did want to know what the heck was going on down there, so I let them put a big mirror at the foot of the bed. Now, Kyle had stayed well north of the equator during this whole time, and he looked like he might be as nauseated as I was, and then I saw why. Birth is supposed to be a magical, beautiful, spiritual experience and everything, but I never want to see the nightmare that was happening to my vagina ever again. Nope, the mirror was quickly taken away and I was back to pushing sans visual aids.

I pushed. I grunted. I screamed like I had never screamed before. I groaned so loudly I would have fit right in on a dairy farm.

And still nothing happened.

Then suddenly, my insides knotted like the ill-advised pretzels I'd snuck earlier, and with the cramps came nausea like I had never experienced. "Puke bucket," I screamed, and started throwing up like I was in *The Exorcist*. I couldn't stop, and as I was puking, I heard Barb say, "It's working, I can see him. Push!"

This was not the magical experience I had envisioned. My mouth tasted like puke. I was sweaty and exhausted and felt as sick as sick could be. I had pooped the bed several times, was shaking uncontrollably, and was screaming like a banshee with every push. Suddenly, the nurse said, "He's sideways. His shoulders are stuck!" Barb had Brexton's head in her hands, Kyle was holding my shoulders for support, and my mom had one of my legs. With the next contraction, the nurse *pushed* hard on my belly with all of her strength, I let out an animalistic grunt, and he was out!

Right away, they placed him on my chest. Kyle and I were crying and laughing and saying hello to our perfect son. We counted ten beautiful fingers, ten perfect toes, two big, chubby cheeks, just like the ones on the figurine my mother found in our yard. It was like my grandmother was there, watching over all of us, and I just knew she was grinning.

So, we had a perfect digit count, a solid size, an adorable face, and . . . a cone-shaped head? Yes, Brexton had spent so much time in the birth canal, his head was shaped like a highway cone. Anxiously, we asked the nurse about it, but she reassured us it wasn't permanent and would go away soon.

As soon as Brexton was on my chest, he stopped crying. There was a holy silence in the room, and the most intense feeling of gratitude I have ever experienced flowed from his warm skin through my entire body. I was crying with joy, radiating love and faith, and everything was perfect in the universe. At this moment, I knew what heaven would be like.

After a few minutes of perfect bliss, Kyle stepped out to share our joy with all our family and friends who had been patiently waiting for hours. I could hear the hoots and hollers from down the hall, and I could feel their love and pride from my bed. Barb came up to me and said she had to tell me something.

"We didn't do an episiotomy because Brexton was supposed to be smaller. But he was almost eight pounds, and you've got a tear."

"A tear?"

"Yes, you ripped a four."

Oh, I thought, *four out of ten isn't bad. They'll just stitch me right up.* Except it was four out of four. I was ripped front to back, from "hole to hole." In fact, it was so bad, it was beyond Barb's ability to stitch, and we had to get a doctor to come in and do it. Luckily, the epidural was still working, because she was stitching down there for what felt like a very long time. As they stitched, Brexton slept on my chest. I kissed his forehead and held him close, just staring at him in awe and wonderment.

The work we had put in, the pain, the labor. The emotional strife, and the physical. Every second of it, every stitch the doctor was putting in where the sun doesn't shine, every shot. Every pimple, every stray hair, every setback. They were all worth it.

With a final tug, the doctor said, "You're all set, Mama."

Mama.

Then it hit me: I was a *mother.*

22

MAKING BREXTON A BIG BROTHER

Brexton was potty trained, sleeping through the night, and able to communicate with us. Gone were the days of lugging half our house with us whenever we had to go somewhere. The never-ending parade of sleepless nights, dirty diapers, and mashed food covering every surface were now replaced with a blissful sleep, cute little Mickey Mouse underwear, and a maturing palate. We'd even seen a recent reduction in the meltdowns that dominate the toddler years, where the tiniest disappointment triggered a volcanic eruption of screams, tears, and "NO!" Instead, we now had a little boy who was full of personality, adventure, and imagination. We had a whole new degree of freedom, and all three of us were thriving.

At the same time, Kyle Busch Motorsports was racking up the Championships in the Truck Series, and Kyle himself was a force to be reckoned with each and every weekend on the track. He was breaking records and setting new ones, and we loved being by his side for all of it. My online boutique was up and running, and staffed with smart, capable women. It was the creative outlet I had been yearning for. Our lives were beautiful, happy, and fun. Now let me tell you, it was a *lot* of hard work, most days from first light until well past dark, but we were achieving everything we set out to do, and seeing our efforts bearing fruit was rewarding.

Our marriage was in the best place it had possibly ever been too; I loved seeing Kyle as a father. He was just the wild dad I'd expected him to be, and Brexton idolized him. In contrast, he was also thoughtful, tender, and even soft in the quiet moments. I watched Brexton teach him the art of flexibility and patience just as Kyle was beginning to teach him the basics of racing, despite my protests about the dangers. The three of us read books together every evening before prayers and bed, and Kyle had a flair for funny voices that made Brexton howl with laughter. As we grew as parents, we grew as partners. Kyle and I had been through an ordeal, and there's something to the saying that what doesn't break you makes you stronger. We learned to appreciate the small moments together maybe even more than the large.

The growing success of the Bundle of Joy Fund was also rewarding. Year after year, we continued to raise awareness about infertility, fight the stigma, and raise more money to help couples find their own Bundles of Joy. Our work caught the eye of the media, and we were inspired that our interviews, discussing the triumphs and tribulations of our journey, could ease the burden others carried. Most important, we received so many applications for grants, and felt so blessed for the small part we played helping other couples realize their dreams of becoming parents. The hardest part was not being able to grant funding to every single couple because each couple was deserving, and every one of their applications touched our hearts. It was their stories that drove us to work so hard to grow the fund. It felt like this was my mission in life. When I was in the darkest parts of my struggle to get pregnant with Brexton, I couldn't figure out why God had burdened me with so much. But now I knew why: I could make a difference in the lives of others. I could help educate other young women on the benefits of being their own advocate. I could help people understand how common infertility is and the importance of supporting people who are facing it. I could help women connect with one another through their shared experiences. I had a voice, and I was learning to use it. It was empowering, and I thanked God every day for the chance to help. We had everything we ever wanted.

Except a daughter.

Month after month, the knowledge that our embryos (although like many in the IVF community, we'd taken to calling them "embabies" by then) were waiting for us called to my heart. One morning, as I watched Kyle and Brexton eating cereal together across the breakfast table, I noticed the one empty chair remaining. I imagined our daughter there, laughing with that perfect glee that only a baby can manage at something one of the boys did, and I knew it was time.

That night, after tucking Brexton in, Kyle and I curled up on the couch. I loved the feeling of his arms wrapped around me, still smelling of our son. I snuggled closer and told him I felt a stirring in my heart that it was time for another baby—the perfect time. He was silent for a minute, and I listened to him breathe as he considered. Kyle does everything fast, and this slow consideration seemed to me to stretch out into an eternity. It never even occurred to me that he might say no, but worry started to bubble up in my stomach as I waited.

"If anyone tries to date her, I'll kill them." He squeezed me tighter as I laughed. We talked late into the night about going through IVF again, discussing how grateful we were to have had multiple embryos, so this time the only part of the process we would face was the embryo transfer. After some back and forth, we also agreed to be very public about the whole process. We wanted to show the world that there was no shame in infertility, and I needed to show other couples who might face the same challenges an honest, intimate view of the process from start to finish. We'd do interviews, but I'd also blog and show videos and really let people into our life. I wanted to be open and accessible to women so that if they had a question, felt like venting, or just needed some encouragement, they'd be able to turn to me. Unlike the last time, we knew what to expect, and instead of uncertainty we could approach it with confidence and humor and show people it's not all sadness and stress. Most important, we would help show people how uniting as partners could help make this arduous journey so much easier to bear.

We called REACH and let them know we were ready to meet our daughter. On the day of the appointment, Kyle and I breezed in, full of confidence and excitement. I was familiar with the medical equipment and the terminology and no longer intimidated by the process, and we thought sharing our experience at the appointment could help others facing their first visit to an infertility clinic.

This first visit back at REACH was a happy affair. We sat with Dr. Wing and Nurse Sue, Mary's replacement. Mary had left the practice since Brexton was born, and we missed her greatly. We were still getting to know Sue but instantly knew she was smart, competent, and calm, with a different energy than our old friend but just as skilled. She asked us if we had decided when we would like to do the transfer.

"Well," I said, "I love a summer birthday, but not too close to Brexton's." As always, we had to keep the NASCAR schedule in mind too, which made things complicated but also excited my love for planning.

"How about looking for a birthday during the August off week?" Kyle suggested. I thought it was perfect. The weather would be warm, it was a whole season after Brexton's special day, and it would give Kyle a week home with us between races. August it was.

Next, we moved on to picking which embaby to implant. Of the three girl embryos we'd had, genetic testing recommended we try either number six or eleven first. "Six," Kyle blurted. "I've got a feeling about six." It wasn't so easy for me. I sat and I struggled for a long time. These two embryos were genetically predestined to be two completely different people, with different ways of thinking, of moving, of speaking, of seeing the world. How was I to choose? How could I possibly have enough information to make the right choice? With Brexton, there was no question. Genetic testing said he was the most viable embryo. That was not the case here.

I envied Kyle's gut reaction, but there was something in my soul that found it so difficult. Of course, there was no wrong answer, and I would love my daughter no matter who she was, but there were two futures playing out in front of me, and I could only pick one. Honestly, it took weeks of me struggling and praying to decide which choice to make. In the end I just couldn't come to any resolution, so I stuck with Kyle's gut feeling.

Finally, right before we left, Dr. Wing called us into his office. He asked how we were doing. We told him how great things were, and about all the new challenges we were taking on. As we talked, I could hear the small "hmm" he made in the back of his throat when he wasn't totally pleased with something. After a minute, he said, "I know how good you both are at managing stress, but remember that the less stress you have in your life, the better environment you are for a pregnancy. Make sure to take time for yourself. Slow down when you can." We promised him we would and headed for home. On the drive home, I added yoga to the nine million things I still had to accomplish that week.

Almost a month later, it was time to start the transfer protocol again. I set my phone up to record a video, and Kyle and I instructed everyone on how to give a shot. Brexton sat next to me on the couch, icing his belly every time I iced mine. His spirit and his humor made this whole process even more exciting, and we spent a lot of time talking with him about how he was going to have a little sister. We were pretty honest about it with him, explaining that soon Dr. Wing would be putting his baby sister in Mommy's belly, where she'd live for nine months before coming out to meet us. He was already in love with her and asked if we could sing her songs to help her go to sleep when she was in my belly. I promised him that we could and that we'd read her stories too. At night, he'd tuck a stuffed animal under his shirt so that he would have a baby in his belly too. He was adorable, and his attentiveness to his unborn sister made my heart swell with love as a mother.

As the shot protocol wore on, we kept having fun! My sister-in-law gave me a shot in a public bathroom during a country music award show, and we posted the video just to show that you can go on living your life. So now I'm on the internet forever, big hair glammed up with long extensions, my green sequined dress hiked up over my belly as my sister-in-law—in her five-inch heels—stabs me in the belly with a needle. I remember her saying beforehand that she'd given a shot to a horse once, so this should be fine.

I can't stress enough the emotional contrast between the second round of IVF prep and the first. Knowing what to expect made it so much less scary, and that's why we wanted to share it with so many people. To be honest, the sharing helped a lot too. I was able to shift my focus outward, away from me and the pressures that came with the process. We were able to shrug off things that brought tears and angst the first time and faced them head-on through the second.

A great example of this came on the day I went in for my trial transfer. This is when they insert the practice catheter to ensure the perfect positioning of the embryo on transfer day. During the procedure, they found a cyst in my uterus. It wasn't dangerous, but it did need to be removed before they could do the transfer. The first time around, this would have crushed me. This time, while there were still a few tears and I was still disappointed, I was able to confront it, schedule the procedure, and move on. I filmed a quick video updating people on our setback. It led to women all over the country messaging me that they'd had the same problems and assuring me their cysts hadn't caused negative effects on their IVF cycles.

During this round, my girlfriends decided to throw me a "Sam's getting knocked up" party. They scheduled a girls' night at my favorite restaurant, where platter after platter of vibrant sushi, the spiciest green wasabi, and cold champagne kept coming. They knew I would soon be missing these things. We laughed and talked late into the night, and all of it felt so good. Here I was, surrounded by my favorite women, about to have a second child with the man I loved more than anything. I wasn't scared this time. I wasn't ashamed. I didn't feel like something was wrong with me as a woman. I was *happy*.

The day soon arrived for the embryo transfer. Kyle and I waltzed into REACH like old pros. We even brought a social media specialist along with us to document the whole process. Kyle's primary NASCAR sponsor is M&Ms, so we came bearing gifts of those sweet candies and stuffed animals for the staff, and they had a surprise for us, too. When Kyle went in to get changed into his hospital garb, instead of the gown he was expecting they handed him a plastic jumpsuit with hand-drawn M&Ms on it to look like the fire suit he wears when racing. We all had a good laugh.

After changing into my own gown, I reached into my purse for my lucky purple transfer socks from the last time, a purple hair tie, and the small plastic baby figurine my mother had found before Brexton was born. I tucked it into the small pocket on the front of the gown, and it felt like Grandma was there with us again. She'd become our guardian angel. I was ready.

This time, when they wheeled me into the room, I had a giant smile on my face. Kyle walked along beside me, smiling almost as widely. Inside was our embryologist, Tyl, Dr. Wing, our nurses, and my social media specialist. I quickly instructed her on which screens in the room to focus on to get the best views of what was happening and then gave everyone big hugs. Together, we said a prayer, asking God for a safe and successful transfer.

Before we knew it, it was done. Our baby girl was inside me, and I promised her I would protect her and keep her safe while she was there. As it had with Brexton, my hand instantly started drifting down to my belly, holding her from the outside, keeping anything bad from happening. We wheeled out to recovery, chatted happily for half an hour, and were on our way home. I didn't even yell too much at Kyle for his driving on the way home, though asking him to drive ten under the speed limit still seemed like a perfectly reasonable request. I spent the next several days taking it easy, without any drama or worry, just pure excitement. Everything felt just like it was supposed to. We'd been down this road before, and this time I was even healthier and stronger than the last. Everything we felt was wrapped in joy and bundled in gratitude.

With the holidays approaching, we felt like Thanksgiving would be the perfect time to let everyone know our transfer was successful. Just like the last time, I jumped the gun, taking a home pregnancy test earlier than I should have. The two bright pink lines told me what I already knew in my soul: I was pregnant with our baby girl. So, a few days before the holiday, we hired a videographer and purchased some pink smoke. We put on our holiday best and even got Brexton a "big bro" T-shirt. As the sun set behind the trees, casting a bright pink glow behind us, we popped the smoke, all three of us laughing and kissing one another in the perfect rose-gold light. It felt like God was there with us, and we were so ready to share all of our love with our baby girl.

Then, we went inside to shoot our Christmas cards. Yes, we're the family who puts up their tree before Thanksgiving. We'd planned to send our announcements to family and friends as our Christmas cards. Everything would be shot in black-and-white, save for a bright pink stocking popping behind us in one photo, and Brexton holding a festive pink box over his head in another T-shirt with "big bro" emblazoned upon his chest. The final photo was of me, hanging a shining pink ornament on the tree. I could feel love radiating from all of us in those pictures when we got the proofs back, and I cried fat, hot tears of joy as I held them in my hands.

23

CRIMSON TEARS

November 27 started out like any other day. I woke up before Kyle and crept quietly out of bed in order to let him sleep. I ate breakfast alone, enjoying the quiet that was rare when a rambunctious toddler is running around the house. But that morning, he was still sleeping. Through my phone, I watched him sleep on our monitor, his hands laced behind his head, mouth gaping open in pure dreaming bliss. I smiled as I ate, imagining what an amazing big brother he would be, and indulged in a little bit of daydreaming. In my mind, I saw him holding her for the first time, sitting on the couch with Kyle helping support her head on his tiny lap. I saw her as a toddler, wobbling after him as he made funny faces and ran away. I imagined him encouraging her as she learned to ride a bike. At each stage in life, I could envision them perfectly, supporting and protecting and loving one another fiercely.

I also used this time to think about how my pregnancy with Brexton went, and how this one might be different. I wondered if some variation in the combination of hormones would change the way I thought, my cravings, or any of the many aspects of pregnancy we don't consider until they happen.

After cleaning up, I went downstairs to work out before my boys woke up. Today was an arm day with a focus on shoulders and a little bit of modified core work. I was energized and happy, performing my exercises as the bright light of the North Carolina sun burst through the windows. It was so great that I didn't have any morning sickness like with Brexton. If it had not been for my boobs being tender and a positive pregnancy test, I would not have thought I was pregnant at all. My mother told me that with my brother, she was sick for almost three months, but with me, she felt bad for under a week and that was it. I crossed my fingers that this ran in the family. Workout over, I wiped the sweat from my forehead with a thick cloth and noticed the smell of bacon filling the house. The boys were up, and I couldn't wait to see them.

After giving both of them a quick kiss good morning and eyeing, with some envy, their plates piled high with syrupy pancakes and crispy bacon, I hopped into a quick shower. My seamstress Tatianna was on her way over to perform my final dress fitting for that weekend's NASCAR awards banquet in Las Vegas. With no need to get dressed up, I pulled on a soft, cream-colored robe and made it downstairs just as the doorbell rang. It was turning out to be a charmed morning, each thing falling into place just as it should.

Tatianna was beaming as she held up a long garment bag and told me she was so excited to share it with me. Excitedly, I rushed her into my walk-in closet, where she unzipped the bag and revealed the dress within. It was *perfect*. The teal satin shimmered in the soft light as she lifted it up. Where there had previously been a puffy lining, there was now just a graceful drape of fabric that I could imagine clinging to my body in all the right places. Newly added rhinestones flashed dazzlingly in the light streaming in from the window, and the formerly conservative gown now had a long slit up the side. Maybe it was the pregnancy hormones, but I was feeling extra sexy and confident these days, and this dress expressed it perfectly.

I stepped into the gown and marveled at how the delicate fabric concealed the tiniest bump that only I would know was there, just below my navel. My breasts, fuller than they had been at the last fitting, strained the bust just enough to accentuate the change without raising eyebrows. As Tatianna pinned away, I daydreamed about the dresses my daughter would someday wear. I pictured her as the flower girl toddling down the aisle in a fluffy white dress adorned with pink flowers at my younger brother's wedding, or shopping for a prom dress with her, envisioning her trying on one sparkly dress after another and looking more beautiful with every twirl. It would be a girls' day out, sharing lunch at her favorite restaurant and making memories that we both would cherish.

It was still early when we finished, and since the only thing I had left to accomplish today was packing for Vegas, I decided to relax with Brexton for a while. We went to his "clubhouse," where we spent some time playing. We took out his favorite dinosaur set and began playing Tyrannosaurus versus Stegosaurus. In his little boy voice, he let out fierce dinosaur roars, and I roared right back. Soon, after the Stegosaurus had been defeated and eaten, we realized it was time to start talking about the humans eating their lunch.

Brexton wanted his favorite dinosaur-shaped chicken nuggets, and I was hoping to talk him into something, anything, else. As we chatted, I noticed some gas pains starting to build in my belly. This wasn't entirely uncommon, and I made a quick trip to the bathroom. I was soon feeling much better. I moseyed back to the clubhouse and cuddled up with Brexton, settling into his reading nook to read *Big Brothers Are the Best*. By the end of the book, my stomach was feeling funny again, and as I bent to put it away the slow build of gas pain became a sudden and powerful cramp, followed by a hot gush of fluid running down my legs. Instantly, my stomach lurched as though I was in an elevator plummeting to the basement.

I was still in my robe, and without thinking I reached down between my legs. My hand came back scarlet, glistening with bright blood. My other hand still held the spine of the book, frozen in time between the perfect morning and a terrifying afternoon. Then, behind the bloody hand, I saw Brexton watching, horror building on his little face. "Mommy, are you hurt?"

Thinking quickly, I said, "Oh, sweetie, I think I cut my hand. Could you run downstairs and get Daddy?" He tore off down the stairs, shouting the whole way. "Dad! Come quick! Mommy's hand is bleeding!"

Almost as quick as my little boy, I ran to the bathroom and tossed the robe on the floor. I sat on the toilet and noticed the red stain still spreading on the cream fabric of my robe. I could feel liquid pouring out of me, an impossible amount. A cold knot of dread pulled itself tight in my soul as the toilet filled with blood. I didn't understand how such a perfect day could have changed so quickly into this nightmare.

Kyle came into the bathroom, expecting to find a cut hand. What he saw drained the color from his face. The bloody robe, me on the toilet, the blood-soaked tissue I had used to clean my legs clutched tightly in my hand. I tried to speak, but no words could make it past the hard lump in my throat. He quickly figured out what was happening and whipped out his phone and told me to call the doctor.

We had REACH on speed dial, and soon a voice I recognized as Sue's came on the line. I tried to speak and nothing happened but a quiet squeak. "Hello?" Sue asked, unsure if she had anyone on the line. Before she could hang up, I tried again and this time the words tumbled out. "It's Samantha Busch. I'm bleeding." Hot tears splashed down my cheeks as the words broke free, the reality of what I feared they meant hitting me as I spoke.

"Don't worry," she said quickly. "A lot of women have periods in their first month of pregnancy."

"It's a lot of blood," I managed.

"What color, and how much?" she asked, all business now.

"It's bright red, and I'm not sure. A lot."

"Are you cramping?" As she asked, it felt like a hot poker was skewering me.

"Yes. Badly."

Quickly, she said, "You need to come in as soon as you can. Today. Now if you can."

As Kyle ushered Brexton into the car, I rushed off to the bedroom to clean up as much as I could and get dressed. While dressing, another strong urge to go to the bathroom came over me. This time, in addition to a gush of blood that made the last one seem like a trickle, there were red, pulpy clots mixed in. I wailed, crying harder than I have ever cried in my life. All of the futures I had just imagined that morning were falling away one by one, leaving a gaping void, and I was teetering on its edge. I was hysterical, tiny gasps of breath coming only when I could force them in. My soul was burning with fear, with confusion, and with a small spark of hope that maybe what I feared was happening was somehow not.

I don't know how much longer it was before Kyle came to find me. When he saw me, sitting on the toilet sobbing out all my pain, he collapsed next to me. We cried together, me begging him to make it stop, to make it all better, and of course he had no way to do that. He stroked my hair, and rubbed my back, and told me he loved me. Eventually, he helped me pull it together enough to get into the car.

The ride was an onslaught of thoughts racing through my mind, panic injecting them with rocket fuel. I thought of proms, and first boyfriends, and her wedding. I loved her so much already, and as each image flashed across my mind's eye it disappeared into the gaping void. It was like the future was a black hole, sucking up from me everything I ever wanted as we flew toward REACH.

I was sitting on a heavy pad, but I could feel blood still flowing out of me. When we reached the clinic and I stood up, I confirmed that not only had it soaked through the pad, it also saturated my pants. I tied a jacket around my waist and hurried inside, where we were quickly ushered to a private room. I found a new pad and excused myself to the bathroom. As I went to sit on the toilet, fiery-red blood splashed onto the floor. A clot the size of a small egg fell off the pad as I pulled down my pants. The sound of it hitting the floor, and the spray of fine red droplets it made on the tiles still haunts me. Some part of me was still rational, and as I knew Dr. Wing would need to examine this, I tenderly gathered it up in the pad, wondering if this was the only time I would hold my baby girl.

My legs, like the bathroom, were now covered in blood. I needed to clean myself up, but if this was my daughter, I didn't want to put her on the floor. I didn't want to put her down ever. So as gently as I could, with tears pouring down my cheeks, I set the bundle down on the small tray bearing specimen cups and other medical supplies. I left her there while I soaked paper towels in warm water and washed the blood off my legs and the floor.

As I tried to gather myself, a gentle knock came at the door, snapping me back to reality. I took a deep, shuddering breath, picked up what I desperately hoped was not my daughter, and left the bathroom. I found Sue, delivered the bundle to her, and explained as calmly as I could what happened. She promised me she would take care of everything, and I went back to Kyle and Brexton. I couldn't tell Kyle what happened because I knew Brexton would hear me and it would scare him. I was scared enough; I didn't want to make him feel what I was feeling. So, I pretended as best I could that nothing had happened and kept reassuring him that we just were here for the doctor to take a little look at Mommy's hand. Soon Sue came in and said maybe it would be better if Brexton waited outside.

She was right, of course. So Kyle packed up our son, my beautiful boy, and brought him over for a kiss. I held him tight, told him how much I loved him, and then they were gone.

I was alone.

24

PAINFUL HOPE

"**You'll need to get changed,**" Sue said as she handed me a too-thin hospital gown. "Take everything off and put this on. Dr. Wing will be in shortly."

She left me alone in the small space with my breath echoing off the linoleum tiles. The ultrasound machine loomed in the corner, a messenger of hope and a harbinger of finality. I hated it. I needed it. I prayed that it would show that my baby was still alive, that somehow the bleeding and the clots and the terror were not me losing the daughter I so desperately wanted.

I avoided looking down as I undressed, not wanting to see how much more I was bleeding. A small red stain had already begun to spread, eclipsing several of the tiny blue diamonds that were decorating the otherwise white gown. I thought I was cried out by this point, but I was wrong.

Easing myself onto the table, I shivered when I touched the icy vinyl surface. It was covered with waxy paper rolled down to protect the table from contamination, and that's how I felt: contaminated, wrong, and untouchable. I wondered how many other women had been here, bleeding their souls onto paper that would erase all signs of their passage to motherhood as soon as they left the room.

It was not long before that I had first positioned myself on this table, overwhelmed with joy at the confirmation of my second pregnancy. I loved the table then—the cold table and crinkling paper were touchstones of what was to come. Now I hated it.

More than anything, I wanted Kyle to be there—but I didn't want Brexton to see this, to know there might be a problem, or to feel any of the fear I felt, so I'd banished Kyle to the warm waiting room outside, where he could watch over our son while I was losing our daughter.

My heart was breaking by the second. Lost in my thoughts, I almost didn't hear the two sharp knocks on the door announcing Dr. Wing's arrival. A gust of warm air from the hallway was cut off abruptly when he stepped in and closed the door. I shivered.

"Hello, Samantha," he said quietly. "Let's see where we are." He walked slowly to the corner of the room and rolled the ultrasound machine beside the bed, one wheel squeaking as it glided toward me. Sue came in behind him, dimming the lights to a near darkness. The sharp white lines on the ultrasound's deep black screen lit up the room with an otherworldly glow, lending sinister shadows to Dr. Wing's always-kind face as he wheeled a small, round stool to the foot of my bed.

I have never been more exposed than I was in this one moment. Although Sue made sure I was covered with rough white towels that smelled strongly of bleach, leaving nothing showing, I still felt completely naked and raw. There was a pressure as Dr. Wing started the exam. Uncomfortably and clinically twisting and turning the probe, he made several "hmm" noises low in his throat. Each "hmm" felt like a death sentence, an unjust declaration

that I was losing my baby. After each move of the probe, he entered information into the machine, its keys thunderous in the small room.

I could see the screen as he examined me, grays and blacks swirling into
dizzying angles and dancing away. I didn't know enough about ultrasounds
to know what I was seeing, so everything looked ominous and everything
looked like salvation. My chest felt tight, and my throat was constricting
around a desperate need to ask what he saw and an unbearable fear of the
answer. I was locked in an impossible moment: I needed to know, and I
desperately didn't want to.

Finally, he removed the probe, its absence suddenly and desperately
missed. Was she in there? Did he see her? Was that the last time I was
going to look for my daughter? I needed the probe back. I needed to find
her. To see. To be her mother.

"I think I see a sac. It's small—much smaller than it should be, but I
think she's still in there . . . it, the baby . . . I mean . . . the fetus."

It was the only time I ever saw Dr. Wing flustered. He's a stoic man, not
unkind, but very matter-of-fact. With Brexton and with this baby, he was
always careful to call my babies "the fetus"—a protection against the uncer-
tainties of pregnancy that I was currently experiencing. His backtracking
and rewording were so unsettling, I had to ask again what he meant.

"So, I'm still pregnant?" Quivering, my voice grabbed on to the finest
threads of hope that his words seemed to deliver.

"Well," he said, "your cervix is closed, so that's good news. I examined
the clot you gave Sue and did not see any obvious fetal tissue. There is a
small sac on the ultrasound, but it is much smaller than we would expect
for this point. And you're bleeding a lot. Much more than we would expect.
At this point, we'll call it a threatened miscarriage. We're going to draw
some labs today and again in a few days to see where your hormone levels
are. Don't give up hope—but I'd prepare for the worst."

That hope, it was the best and worst thing I had ever heard. I came in
knowing I'd lost my baby. Now I didn't know if I had or if I had not—and

I wouldn't know for a few more days. I had something to cling to, but was it futile? If I was still pregnant, what did that mean for my baby? If the pregnancy continued, would she be healthy? Would she be safe?

But he also didn't say I wasn't pregnant! He didn't say I'd lost my baby. He said it was a *threatened* miscarriage, not a definite one. In that moment, I resolved to fight for my daughter. To believe in her. To cling to those gossamer strings of hope for as long as they would carry me.

If only I knew how to do it.

Dr. Wing patted my hand and stepped out of the room. Sue helped me sit up and told me I could get dressed. She said she'd be back in a few minutes with someone to draw blood, and in a moment, I was alone again. I took a deep breath of the cold, sterile, medical air and tried to slow my heart.

I was pregnant.

I was not pregnant.

I was a flipping coin, tumbling through the air, two possibilities replacing each other, never settling on one answer. How would the coin land?

I put my clothes back on and tried to figure out how to face Kyle and Brexton in my new, uncertain state.

25

SHATTERED DREAMS

I spent the drive home in stunned silence. Brexton asked if my hand was better, and I told him that yes, Dr. Wing fixed it right up, facing forward and crying as silently as possible. It felt like a certainty that I miscarried, but we didn't know for sure, and I didn't want to have to tell him anything until we did know. I hated that sliver of hope, burning deep against the ice in my heart. It felt like poison; it felt like salvation.

Once we were home, there was nothing to do but wait. I sat on the couch, blank, staring at my phone on the table and dreading the call I knew was coming. Absently, I'd check the clock every hour to find only minutes had passed since the last time I checked. Time was broken, like me. Minutes passed inside every second, and hours in every minute. Kyle took Brexton upstairs to play while I waited. When the phone finally rang, my heart tumbled into a deep hole and I had to force my hand to pick it up.

"Hello?" Even to my own ears, my voice sounded flat and distant, as though someone else was speaking.

"Samantha, it's Sue from REACH. Is now a good time to talk?" I told her it was and braced for the bad news.

"Well," she started, "your pregnancy hormones have actually increased since the last time we had you tested. When we drew your blood last week, you were at 4,000. Now you're at 7,000. We'd like to see them much higher, but since they've increased, we can't confirm anything yet. We want you to stay on your shot regimen for now and come back in for blood work in forty-eight hours."

I was stuck in limbo again. If my pregnancy hormones kept going up, it meant I was still pregnant. If they dropped, it meant I'd miscarried. There was nothing to do but wait. I was so damn sick of waiting. The burning shard of hope in my heart flared up, and I hated it. It brought desperation, and it would bring so much more pain if I did lose my little girl.

Of course, this was the day we were supposed to fly to Las Vegas for the NASCAR banquet on Thursday night. I had a few short hours to figure out if I was even going to go. Ultimately, I felt like I did not want to be alone with my thoughts and my pain. I needed Kyle, my rock. I didn't want to get the results of my next blood test while I was alone. Kyle agreed, and soon we were dropping Brexton off with Mom and Pops and heading to the airport.

I barely remember the flight or that night as we got to the hotel. I remember praying with Kyle, on our knees together in the room, with our hands clasped together, pleading with God to let me keep her and telling Him how much we loved her. Eventually, we ran out of words but stayed there with the carpet making red indents on our knees, praying silently with our hearts when we had nothing left to say.

Thursday morning came with an unexpected sense of optimism. I was out of the depths of the despair I'd felt the night before and was ready to do the thing I always do when faced with a problem: research. Before

Kyle woke up, I was sitting at the small table in our hotel with my phone, searching for any scrap of information I could find about similar situations. It turned out that in about 50 percent of cases, pregnancies progressed normally. The hope that burned too hot yesterday now blossomed, and I welcomed it. Maybe this was just a really bad scare but would turn out okay. I held on to hope with everything I had.

Kyle woke, and we went out to a nearby diner for breakfast. Over a huge platter of omelets and pancakes, the sweet scent of maple syrup floating up off my plate, Kyle shared his own optimism. "I really believe this is just a scare. We've been through too much." I told him what I had learned that morning, and he smiled so brightly the Vegas lights seemed dim by comparison. "See? It's going to be okay!"

It helped that I wasn't bleeding or cramping anymore and hadn't been since that terrifying trip to REACH. I rubbed my belly lovingly, talking to a baby girl I was coming to believe was still there, pouring love and calm and protection and faith into my womb. Yesterday, the hours refused to pass. Today, they rushed on like sunrise, shining more and more hope as they went on. Stuffed to the gills, we left the restaurant and went to get my blood drawn. I was so hopeful that I barely even flinched when they poked the sharp needle into the crook of my elbow and drew off several tubes of thick, dark blood. It was sent off in an envelope marked "STAT," telling the lab to rush the news back to us.

This buoyant feeling stuck with me throughout the day. It was almost an elation, like the feeling after surviving a car wreck. I felt like I had been on the sharp edge of something impossibly tragic and had come out all right. No matter how hard it was, I was committed to fight through whatever came, and I knew in my heart my little girl was a fighter.

Late in the afternoon, my hair and makeup artist, Krystal, arrived. We'd known each other for years, and as she went to work, I filled her in on what was happening. She shared my optimism, and told me she believed everything would be fine too. As she curled my hair, she shared a story of a woman she knew who went through a similar experience. Her son was now four, healthy and full of life. She was applying finishing touches, just half an hour before I was to be on the red carpet, when my phone rang. We locked eyes, both knowing that the call was my results. She picked it up off the counter and handed it to me.

As it vibrated in my palm, I wasn't sure if the phone or my hand was shaking more. In my head, I scripted out how the call was going to go. "Samantha, it's Sue," she'd say, with relief thick in her voice. "Your numbers are great! This was just a scare. Take it as easy as you can, and we'll have you in for a follow-up when you get back." In my head, I thanked her for her kindness.

When I answered, though, her voice told another story. It was low, serious, and sad. "I'm so sorry, Samantha." Like my heart, my pregnancy hormones had plummeted. What was 7,000 earlier was 2,000 today. It was official, I was no longer pregnant.

My baby girl was gone.

26

INCONSOLABLE

Perhaps the hardest part of the days following my miscarriage came immediately after receiving the news. In less than half an hour, we needed to be on the red carpet for the NASCAR awards banquet, smiling for the cameras, doing interviews, making small talk with people in the industry, and trying to celebrate that year's NASCAR champion, who was the focus of the night. I didn't even have thirty minutes to grieve, which was a blessing and a curse. The realities of the time pressure meant I was able to compartmentalize just enough to get through. I didn't want to face the news or to think about it yet; to do so would mean that it was real and true. I needed to be presentable, to have hair and makeup that didn't look like I had just lost a baby. I wanted to hold on to the idea that it wasn't true, that she was still with me for a bit longer. But I had, and everything that was important inside me seemed to die with her.

When I hung up the phone, Krystal squeezed my hand tightly, sharing silently in a moment of intense pain, and her kindness made it a bit less lonely. With a silent nod, I let her finish my face with my eyes dry as sand. If I let the tears come now, they would never stop, and if I stopped going through the motions, I would have to face the horrific truth. I looked at my dress hanging limply beside her. I had chosen it specifically for how it would look on my pregnant body, clinging just slightly to the still-tiny baby bump and my swelling breasts. Except now there was no baby.

When Krystal was done, she gave me a quick, close hug and silently packed her things. There was no space in the room for the idle, fun chit-chat of before. The air was filled with an oppressive emptiness, and I'm not sure sound would have been able to cut through it. I found Kyle in the bedroom, freshly showered and shaved and getting himself dressed. In a matter-of-fact voice, I told him Sue had called.

"The numbers confirm the miscarriage. I'm not pregnant anymore."

"Oh, Sam," he started, but I cut him off.

"I don't want to talk about it. I can't. I'm not going to cry. I'm not ready to accept this. We're going to the banquet, and we'll pretend nothing is wrong." The thought of staying in the room alone left my chest twisted with panic, and my absence from the banquet would have been noticed. Kyle would have been asked over and over again why I wasn't there, and it wasn't fair to make him carry that weight by himself.

The hot ember of hope that was burning in my chest all day was now a glacier: slow, huge, cold, and impenetrable. If I was frozen, I couldn't feel. I could be numb. No tears flow from a glacier, just hard, blue ice. When Kyle tried to hug me, I floated away. Glaciers don't need comfort, and to them, warmth is deadly.

Downstairs, I held stoic through the event. We'd *just* announced our pregnancy on social media a few days ago, and friends seeing me for the first time came to congratulate me on my pregnancy. I smiled at them, my frozen eyes never catching the mirth. I thanked them, every kind word and celebratory hug hardening the icy core in my spirit. I posed for pictures, an entirely fake smile plastered on my face to cover the madness trying to escape behind it.

Throughout the night, Kyle was affectionate and attentive, clearly worried about me and suffering himself, but I couldn't meet his eyes or the glacier would shatter and the careful, tenuous facade would crumble. After the banquet, we made it back to the room. I undressed with robotic hands, removed my makeup, and lay back on the bed without saying a word. Kyle got in next to me, both of us lay flat on our backs staring at the ceiling, and he turned off the light. I was certain I would never sleep again—glaciers didn't need sleep either—but a sudden and deep exhaustion soon consumed me, and I fell into a dreamless slumber.

It happened at 2:00 AM. The glacier exploded, and each sharp shard of ice cut and tore as it shot through me. I flew out of bed and sat in the corner of the room, my back pressed into the wall and my knees drawn up tight against my chest. I wrapped my arms around them, and I wailed. It was the soul torment of a suddenly childless mother. It was primal. It was the cry of mothers around the world when they outlive one of their children, the unfathomable pain of having someone you love beyond measure ripped out of your life. My mind kept replaying the week's events in short flashes, a kaleidoscope of trauma. "Mommy cut her hand," shouted Brexton, the bright red blood dotting the bathroom floor. Dr. Wing saying he thought he saw a sac. Sue telling me that my numbers had increased, and the giant clot flashed over and over again. That night, I learned what hell is like . . . torture and agony.

By this point it was early morning on the East Coast, and I started texting Sue at REACH. "How did I cause this?"

"You didn't cause this, Samantha. I promise. Sometimes this just happens."

I asked her about flying, and working out, and every single thing I did that now overwhelmed me with shame. Each time, she told me how it was not anything I'd done and explained why. Intellectually, I understood what she was saying, but her words made no sense. *I was her mother.* It was my job to take care of her, to keep her safe, to be her home, to protect her, but I had failed in those most basic responsibilities, and now she was gone. I wanted to tear myself apart. I didn't deserve her.

My anguish woke Kyle, and as he sat up sleepily from bed, I saw Brexton's face in his. "Oh, God," I cried, "how are we going to tell Brexton?" A vise squeezed my chest, and I struggled to breathe. Since he learned to talk, Brexton had been asking us for a brother or sister. He was so excited, and now I was going to have to rip that away from him. I failed my daughter, and now I realized how I had failed my son, too. My despair deepened, and Kyle and I spent the rest of the night pressed together crying in the corner.

As the Nevada sun started to brighten the room, my phone started to chime. Texts from around the country as more people saw my original announcement that we were pregnant. Each one was a spear, plunging deep into my heart. Every comment on the social media posts about our daughter burned like hellfire. I knew we were going to have to make an announcement about what happened because I could not bear the weight of the well wishes. But I also wasn't ready to take that step, to hold the weight of all that sympathy. I was stuck. Instead, I uploaded a video from a few days earlier when we'd learned we had a threatened miscarriage.

That day, I found a video that gymnast Shawn Johnson made after she suffered a miscarriage. It started with Shawn and her husband explaining that this wouldn't be a happy video, but that they hoped it would make other people feel less alone. Right away, this resonated because there was a vast desert of loneliness in the middle of what I was experiencing. The video continued as a collection of clips telling the story of their pregnancy. Shawn cried happy tears after learning she was pregnant, surprising her husband with the news and a pair of baby shoes. Then Shawn on the phone with her doctor, explaining cramping and bleeding *just like* the cramping and bleeding I'd had. Her husband telling her everything was going to be okay, *just like* Kyle had said to me. Her doctor confirmed right away that she had miscarried, and she'd been shattered, *just like* I was right then. My heart broke for her, but I also felt a pang of jealousy that they never had to bear the false hope Kyle and I had. I didn't know if it was worse to have that hope and lose it or to have never had it at all.

So, I turned on my camera, not knowing if it was going to see the light of day, and hit *Record*. I poured it all out, telling the story in brutal detail. I said I didn't know where we would go from here. I didn't know what was going to happen. I didn't know how to put the pieces back together. I didn't know what I'd do if I lost her. I don't know, I don't know, I don't know, over and over and over again. I needed the release of saying it, of getting it all out of my body.

I wasn't ready to make a new video, telling the end to the story, but I wanted to put this out into the world, so I uploaded it to Instagram. Then I called my mom and told her the news. She cried with me and said all the right things, and so did the few close friends I called and told. The problem is the right things aren't right *enough*. They can't assuage the hurt. As I hung up the phone after the last conversation, I was spent. I couldn't talk anymore, so I turned off my phone.

Later that morning, Kyle and I drove two hours into the desert to the sand dunes where we would spend a few days before going back to face the world. We spent a few hours driving through the dunes in a blissful silence as the wind and sand swirled around us and resting in the RV between bouts of deep sadness. Then the cramps started again, followed by more bleeding. I knew what was happening, and it pulled me right to the edge of insanity. With the bleeding came clots, and I knew one of those clots would contain my daughter, and I didn't know what to do. I couldn't just flush them. Should I bury them? Do I pray? Should I dissect them and look for her body to have a funeral? Would I even know what an embryonic sac looked like if I found it? I wrapped each one in toilet paper and then a paper towel. The blood soaked through the collection, staining my hands and crusting under my nails. Finally, I laid them gently in the trash.

In the trash, I chided myself. *What kind of mother are you?* But I couldn't find a better solution. I also couldn't find a solution for telling Brexton. I just couldn't take ripping his little heart out the way mine had been ripped from me. I couldn't face him with all my shame and guilt. And then there was Kyle, who I could tell was sad but who was not broken in the way I was. I was angry at him for being stoic. I could tell he hurt for me and wanted to help, but what I needed was for him to burn in the same anguish I was burning in. I needed to see that his soul was on fire the way mine was. Logically, I appreciated that he was holding it together and handling it with grace for the family, but when he said, "The situation sucks, but there's nothing we can do to change or fix it," I was dumbstruck. *Why was it so much easier for him than for me?*

When we returned home, I knew it was time to tell Brexton. I felt like I had cried all the tears I had, and it was a wonder the sand dunes weren't now a lush oasis from all the water I provided them. I thought I would be able to hold it together long enough to tell him the truth. Kyle and I brought him into his room and told him we had some news to share.

When Kyle and I first started shots in preparation for embryo transfer, Brexton named his sister "Doinkey." He would go around the house, saying, "This is where we can put Doinkey's high chair," or "Here is where Doinkey's diapers will go!" At night, he would read a bedtime story to her, kiss my belly, and say, "Sweet dreams, Doinkey. I love you." And so, we simply told him that his baby sister, Doinkey, was not in Mommy's belly anymore, that she was in heaven with God. My voice quaked, and I rubbed his little back as I spoke. He was quiet for a moment, processing, and then leaned over, kissed my belly, and said, "Goodbye, Doinkey. I love you."

We were shocked at how well he was handling it, no tears, almost as if he had known already. We explained to him that he would have been an amazing big brother to her, and that now she would be watching down over him. With inquisitive eyes, he looked at Kyle and asked why God needed Doinkey to go to heaven and be an angel. "I don't know, buddy," he replied, "maybe someday you can ask Him." Brexton considered this, his little face serious and pensive. As he thought, we told him it was okay if he felt sad or angry or wanted to cry or didn't feel anything at all. He said he was sad he wouldn't get to play with her but seemed okay.

In the days that followed, he'd often ask if God was ready to send Doinkey back from heaven yet, and every time, it broke my heart. How can you explain to someone who hasn't yet lived half a decade what *forever* meant? When you're three, *later* and *forever* are the same thing.

The days started to run together, and it got harder and harder to find any joy at all. The sense that everyone was walking on eggshells around me was maddening, so I plastered on the facade I wore that night at the NASCAR banquet. I tried to laugh and joke and be my old self, but the smiles never made it farther than my lips. I would play with Brexton right up until bedtime, say our prayers, and get him tucked in. But as soon as I turned out his lights, it was like I'd flipped a switch on myself as well. I'd spend hours each night in the bedroom crying. I was so frustrated with my body. Not only could I not get pregnant without medical help, now I couldn't even carry a baby once I got that help. I felt like I was being pressed under a heavy stone; each breath became a struggle; each day I was a little flatter.

Christmas came like a cruel joke. Families sent Christmas cards, with pictures of smiling babies and families with new members from last year's card. Each one was a dagger, and even the story of the Nativity and the birth of Jesus seemed designed to cause me suffering. Our own batch of 250 cards, full of pink ornaments and stockings and presents to announce our daughter, sat on a counter mocking me until I threw them all in the trash in a fit of rage.

Each day was more robotic, a routine of going through the motions, but there was nothing there of *me*. I had become a shell of Samantha, a look-alike with no soul. I felt monumentally alone, abandoned by God and everyone who loved me. Their reticence to hurt me, the sense that they were not being themselves for fear of making things worse for me, just left me feeling even more isolated. This fed into a negative energy loop, with me convinced nobody should want to be around me given how broken I was. I was so raw that any contact, anything close, caused a flare of new pain.

I poured myself into Brexton, probably too much. I didn't want to miss a single thing. It was overcompensating for what I viewed as my failure. We built massive forts out of every pillow in the house, made the messiest projects he wanted to do, and took daily ice cream runs. I smothered him with kisses and hugs, touching him every second I could. I developed a deep-seated fear about something happening to him, and it sometimes left me paralyzed. If he got in a car with anyone but me driving him, I paced back and forth like a caged tiger until I got the call that they'd made it to their destination. Every night, I woke Kyle as I cried out in nightmare-driven terror.

My love for Brexton was the one bright light, a lifeboat in a raging ocean, and I clung to it for dear life. At the same time, my failure to give him a little sister made me physically ill. His "big bro" shirt lay folded in the bottom of a drawer in his dresser, and I imagined him taking it out and looking at it when we weren't there. I hated that I couldn't give this to him, when I would do anything to make him happy. It deepened my sense of failure, and the storm continued to rage.

27

WHERE PATHS CROSS

We needed to do something differently. Each day was more agony, pushing me further from my family hour by hour. I clung to Brexton unhealthily, forcing him to endure long hugs, sitting in his room watching him sleep for hours as tears rolled down my cheeks. With Kyle I was fine one minute—we would be back to our normal, loving banter—and I was sobbing on his shoulder the next. I stopped calling friends, convinced nobody would want to talk to me in the state I was in, and just as convinced I didn't want to talk to anybody either.

The onslaught of Christmas parties was the absolute worst. People would express sympathy, meaning well but just torturing me. When one friend told me she had also endured a miscarriage, I breathed a sigh of relief, thinking I had found someone who would get it. Then she went on to tell me how she felt like she had dodged a bullet, because the kids she had were so great and "those babies were probably bad apples" anyway, and

I raged inside again as a plastic smile sat unmoving on my face. The line of women who made flippant or minimizing remarks burned at my core: "At least you weren't that far along"; "Everything happens for a reason"; "I had a friend who couldn't get pregnant and when she finally stopped thinking about it, it happened." Each remark diminished my pregnancy or placed blame on me in a passive-aggressive way. All the decorations and cheer, the celebrations of new beginnings that came with the new year, and even a fresh blanket of white snow deepened my depression until I felt like I would never, could never, be healed.

So, we decided to take a trip to the Bahamas, our happy place. Normally, we would bring friends and family with us, partying long into the night and finding fun things to do during the day, but not this time. It would be a chance to heal, to escape from the demands of everyone else and to focus on our little family. When we arrived, the salt air was an immediate balm, transporting me away from the troubles of home and giving me a small spark of much-needed happiness. It felt like a part of me was reawakening.

That's when a flu hit. For two days, wracked by aches, chills, and fever, I slept. Quarantined to a separate bedroom, my exhausted body shut down. It was like the torment of my soul manifested in my body, and the only response I had to it was to sleep it off. I would wake every few hours to sweat-soaked sheets and drink huge gulps of water through parched lips before passing back out. I was miserable, but the physical agony gave me a different focus from my spiritual torment. It was almost welcome, a reminder that I was still alive. When I slept, I did not dream. This alone was a change—most nights before I got sick, I dreamt that I'd lost Brexton in a morbid kaleidoscope of soul-crushing ways that left me paralyzed with fear even after I awoke.

When the fever finally broke on the third day, I felt reborn. My body, bereft of true sleep for almost a month, was newly rested. With that came the chance to see the world through new eyes. I vowed to climb out of the pit of darkness rung by rung until I crested its rim and stepped off the ladder into the bright sun. The next few days were spent swimming and playing with Brexton and focusing on reconnecting mentally and physically with Kyle after so many nights of tears and support, and I had the first genuine laughs since losing the baby. Of course, this sparked more confusion as it felt like a betrayal of my daughter to feel happy now, but I did my best to stay in the moment because my family deserved the best of me.

The day before we left, Kyle and Brexton were napping, exhausted after our full day of swimming in the warm, blue sea. I looked in on them, mouths open and eyes closed, and smiled. I decided to take advantage of the quiet and go for a walk on the beach. Since the miscarriage, I had been desperate to be alone yet terrified of being alone with my thoughts. Now was the first time to do that, and I felt like I might be ready.

I quietly closed the door and stepped out onto the soft white sand. The gentle pulse of the ocean waves, hissing as they came up onto the beach, was a calming whisper that accompanied me as I started to walk. I wanted everything to go back to the way it had been before the miscarriage, but I didn't know how to get there. I felt fundamentally changed by this experience. I knew I was being unfair to Brexton and Kyle, not being there 100 percent, but it also felt like a betrayal of my little girl to be happy. And what about me? How could I be fair to myself when I was stuck blaming myself for something that I knew wasn't my fault?

I was so lost in my thoughts that I was startled when I reached the end of the beach. A thick tangle of dune grass and rocks blocked the path, and the soft white sand turned to gravel beneath my feet. When I turned to go back, I was granted a miracle. The beach was deserted; all the joggers and swimmers and vacationers had departed. Deep purples and fiery oranges flared from the western sky as the blue deepened to indigo above me. The sun was setting in a vista of such pure beauty that joy bubbled out of my mouth in an explosion of grateful laughter. Out over the ocean, a flock of bright white seagulls was flying parallel to the coast, pointing my way back to my family. Earlier, two planes had traversed the sky, and their contrails formed a giant pink cross reflecting the light of the sunset across the sky. That cross glowed into my soul.

I knew this was a sign from God and from my daughter. It felt like she was saying, "Mommy, don't be sad. I'm in heaven. I'm safe and happy, and you should be too." Happy tears streaked down my face, and I sat in the sand watching the beautiful pink cross slowly fade from the evening sky. I prayed to God that He would help heal my heart and take good care of my little girl. I prayed He would help make me stronger from this experience and be the mother and wife my family needed me to be. Finally, I begged Him with all my soul to let her know how much she would be loved and missed. When I was finished praying, I traced my single line of footsteps back to my boys.

I focused on the sound of the ocean, the truly awe-inspiring sunset, and the smell of the tropical air as I walked, feeling warmth inside me for what felt like the first time. This beauty was as close to heaven as there was on earth, and I knew my daughter was in a place even more beautiful, waiting for me. Even though I longed to hold her, to cover her in kisses, and to tell her how much I loved her, I found peace in this knowledge.

I wasn't yet healed, but I had finally started healing.

28

PLANTING REMEMBRANCE

Early that spring, after we got back from the Bahamas, things were strained in my life. Like I said, I was healing but not yet healed. I felt a desperate need for community. It was such a lonely place to be, and I wanted to connect with women who understood how I felt during a time when my husband and the other people who were normally closest to me were not able to.

Over the years, I'd become close with women around the world who were also experiencing infertility and IVF. I was outspoken in the community and always tried to be a shoulder for people who needed one, and a friend to anyone who came looking for friendship. Through so many late nights, I virtually held women's hands as they poured their hearts out to me.

Now I needed to lean on these women. I needed their shoulders, their ears, their hearts. In the shared pain of our loss, we were bound together as tightly as family. They *understood* that being six weeks along in an IVF pregnancy was a big deal, and not something to "just get over." They knew the struggle of genetic testing and the confidence received from it, the stresses of nonstop doctors' appointments and daily shots. Some of them understood the immense joy of learning that finally, after so much strife, you were pregnant. And some knew the pain of losing that pregnancy scant weeks later. Each of them listened to me the way I'd listened to them. Through Instagram messages and emails with anonymous women I will never meet, I shared my deepest secrets, fears, and insecurities. They allowed me space for my pain and did not shy away from it. Ultimately, they were able to provide me with what I craved so desperately: validation. They reaffirmed that I was allowed to be sad, that grieving was normal, and that even when the people who loved me didn't understand, it didn't mean I wasn't understandable.

The physical distance from these women itself was a balm. Sometimes, with the people in my life, the love and pity in their eyes was too much for me to bear, and I would shut down. I didn't always *want* to be held, and hugging is what people do to assuage the pain of people near them. I was always afraid of putting too much of my own burden on the people in my immediate sphere. With this amazing community of women, complete strangers in most cases, these reservations melted away. I was able to express myself fully, without fear of judgment or pity or pushing anyone away. They were there for me in such a powerful way, and I will always be grateful to them for that.

I was talking to one of these women, explaining how I just wanted some way to find closure. I felt like, since we had no funeral for our baby, no ceremony to mark her life, it was almost like her life didn't matter. She suggested planting a tree in our daughter's honor—something she had done to remember her son. I loved the idea of putting vibrant, growing life in the world in her name and having a physical reminder of her presence.

This could be the memorial we never had, a chance to say goodbye and help my heart heal just a little more.

I decided on a cherry tree, whose bright pink and white blossoms would blaze forth every spring. The spot we chose was just outside our bedroom window, where I would always be able to see it. The day we selected for the planting was warm and sunny, and a gentle breeze blew through our hair as we walked through the green grass of our yard to where the tree stood. Kyle, Brexton, Mom, Pops, and I all dressed up for the occasion. I chose a bright white dress emblazoned with a swirl of colors, which reminded me of the Bahamian miracle sky. I didn't want to remember my baby girl in black. The vibrant dress was an expression of the happiness her presence brought me rather than the sadness of her absence.

I had tasked each member of the family with putting down some words to say as we gathered. *The chance to come together and speak our pain would be cathartic,* I thought. Brexton went first, placing a drawing he made of hearts covered with glitter, a tall yellow sunflower, and his best "I love you, Doinkey" scrawled across the top. He placed it in the freshly shoveled earth so that he and Doinkey would always be connected. Then it was Kyle's turn.

I was nervous as he opened his mouth to speak. I was afraid I would hear some of the resentment that I was starting to sense building between us in his voice. But he was amazing. His words were brief but heartfelt, and maybe pulled us a little closer together. As the warm spring breeze ruffled his hair, he spoke.

"We'll forever cherish you for how you were created," he started, emotion thick in his voice, "and having gone through all the things we did to create you. We miss you every day and will forever carry you in our hearts till we get to meet you again in heaven." Tears were pouring down my face as he finished, "Love, Dad." After placing his note on the ground at the base of the new tree, he picked Brexton up on his shoulders. Their shadows stretched together to wrap around the silvery-gray trunk of the tree.

Then it was my turn. Taking a deep breath, I struggled to read the message I held in my shaking hands. This was so hard, but necessary. I steadied myself, and with a strong but tight voice, I started to read. "To my sweet baby girl, you were loved tremendously, and I prayed for you every night long before we even began the process to have you." It became harder to speak with every word, tears closing my throat against the sobs trying to burst through. But I needed to get the words out. "Your brother was so excited to meet you. It's amazing how in terms of time, you were only with me briefly. But the love I have for you is so overwhelming. You were loved in a way that is hard to put into words. For someone so very little, you left the biggest hole in my heart."

I felt Brexton's tiny hand, reaching down from his perch on Kyle to rub my shoulder. Then, Kyle's hand followed, supporting me through my pain. I did not shy away from their touch—not today. With the three of us connected, and our daughter's presence there in our space too, I finished. "Not a day will go by that I won't think of you until we meet again one day. Sweet baby girl, know that you have a mommy, daddy, big brother, and a family that loves you so much, and your memory will never fade from our hearts." I cried then, letting it all out, before placing my note and a flower with Kyle's and Brexton's at the base of the tree.

Mom and Pops finished their farewells, and after standing there together for a few minutes, the sun began to set. Soon, Kyle and Brexton went up into the clubhouse to play, and Mom and Pops headed back to their house. I took a moment alone to say a more private goodbye. I knelt down in the fresh soil and mulch forming a rich brown ring around the tree, put my hands on the ground, and cried. Pink light streaked across the western horizon as the sun dipped ever lower, and the spring breeze lifted to a stronger gust. I told my baby how much I missed her, and how I would be there to hold her in heaven just as soon as I was called home.

I would be lying if I said this was the true closure I needed. Hearing Kyle speak, feeling the connection with my family, and saying the words that were in my heart helped, but it's also true that losing a child takes a piece of your heart, and it will be missing forever. But, on the days that are hardest, I go and sit by the tree. I touch its bark, look at its thin branches stretching up to the sky, and imagine her there with me. In this way, she's always with me.

29

IMPLODING AND REBUILDING

After the tree planting, I started to feel like I was finding my way back to myself. It's not that I never cried or felt sad, because I did. There would still be days when I felt like I needed to distance myself from others, but the bouts were spaced out and no longer an everyday occurrence. And the sadness was not as raw. I missed my daughter and the feel of my pregnant body reminding me that she was there. I missed the future I'd imagined for her, but my sorrow started to change from desperation to wistfulness, a sweet ache in the center of my soul.

The new NASCAR season was under way, and the constant work that comes with the season provided me with a healthy focus for my mind and my energies. Between the travel, running the boutique, managing the foundation and blog, and raising an almost-four-year-old, I was at full tilt.

There were still days when something would trigger a flash of sadness, and the tears would flow again. Most of the time, this would pass quickly with a silent round of tears, but one particular picture of a newborn baby girl on Instagram pushed me past the gentle crying into a bout of sobbing. Lying next to me in bed, playing on his phone, I heard Kyle let out a sigh.

"What?" I asked, thinking he had seen something frustrating online.

"Are you crying again?" His harsh tone was like a slap, echoing off the walls.

Fresh tears sprung from my eyes, and I lashed back. "Well, excuse me for being sad over a huge loss!"

"I thought you were over all of this," he barked. "You were only six weeks, Samantha. It sucks, I'm sorry it happened, but it's time to get over it already."

Flabbergasted, I asked, "Do you think I *want* to feel like this? Do you think I like this?"

"Whatever." He rolled over and turned his cold back to me, switching off the light with his breath coming in short, angry bursts in the sudden darkness.

I felt like he had punched me in the gut. The man I loved and had built a life with had literally turned his back on me. Fear and confusion flooded in behind the sadness. I reminded myself that everyone fights, and that nobody is always perfect. I calmed myself down so I could go to sleep, confident we'd talk about it in the morning and work it out like we always did. Boy, was I wrong.

The months that followed were some of the hardest I've endured. The man I married often seemed to be nothing but anger and resentment, all aimed at me. Where we used to support each other, it felt like he was actively willing me to fall. Small fights and minor annoyances became shouting matches, and any little spark would turn the dry tinder of our relationship into a roaring fire. One afternoon another one of these fights was brewing. I was trying to talk it through over and over, and he was shutting down, hopping on his phone, ignoring my pleas. Tensions were palpable. Frustrated, I decided to take Brexton out to the Children's Museum, hoping some physical space would help cool things down.

We'd been there a few hours, Brexton laughing at his reflection in fun-house mirrors and blowing giant bubbles from a bright yellow wand, when Kyle texted me to apologize. "I'm sorry for the way I treated you," he said. Well, I was still too hurt, and an apology over text wasn't going to cut it, so I ignored it. Kyle happened to be racing that night, and by the time we got back to the motorhome there was only time for a quick dinner before heading to the track for the driver introductions. Kyle was back to not speaking to me at all, and I wasn't budging either. This was not something a few quick texts could solve. I was shocked at how unlike us we had become. Usually, we were able to communicate and treat each other with respect, and this felt foreign and bad.

Still, I went to the pit box to watch the race, and I'd cheered as Kyle ended up winning. I went to the winner's circle to give him a kiss. He turned his face away, and under his breath asked, "Why are you even here? I don't want to see you."

Shocked, I took Brexton back to the motorhome to stew while Kyle had his media obligations after the race. I was furious, and waiting stoked that fury into a rage. I replayed the day over and over again in my head, trying to find the moment when things had gone so wrong. When Kyle came in, I was reading a book to Brexton. I didn't want to fight in front of him, so I ignored Kyle and kept on reading. Something in the story made Kyle snicker, and I could feel him looming in the doorway.

"What?" I asked curtly, glaring up at him from behind the colorful pages.

"What are you doing here reading? I told you I didn't want to see you." A cold scorn hung off his words, thick and acrid as poison.

"Where do you want me to go, Kyle?" I asked hotly.

"Not my problem," he spat, the harsh words shooting out like chips from a woodsman's axe.

"Grow up, Kyle. Stop fighting in front of Brexton. It's not like there's anywhere for me to go in a 500-square-foot motorhome." I was incredulous.

"No, Samantha," he almost smiled behind the derision. "I want you to leave. I'm sick of you."

"I'm not going anywhere," I flung back. "Stop talking like a jerk in front of Brexton." Our son had gone silent and still, staring at his parents with wide, frightened eyes.

"Oh, like that's any worse than your damn crying in front of him all the time?" Every word was a splinter dug deep into my skin, burning.

"Watch your language," I screamed at him, and we were off to the races. We were both shouting, saying things we would never have said to each other just a few short months before. I finally just stopped responding and got Brexton ready for bed. I tucked him in with a fake smile, and I promised him everything was going to be okay. "Mommy and Daddy were just having an argument, but it will be better soon." But of course, it didn't get better. With Brexton asleep, I begged and pleaded with Kyle to end his sudden aggression toward me, and he would either shout back or completely ignore me. We went to bed with nothing resolved and no plan to make it better.

This was in March, and it was the start of a three-week road swing on the West Coast. We would be spending a lot of time together, and I thought we would talk and find our way through it, as we always had during the decade we'd been together, but it wasn't happening. I kept pleading with Kyle to explain his moods and his treatment of me, and he'd snort back with retorts like, "*My* moods? Try living with you, crying all the time. That's real fun."

These conversations would spin around and around like a CD on repeat until Kyle stormed out of the room. I was crushed and felt that I'd not only lost my baby, but I'd lost the man I loved, my best friend, and the most steadfast support I'd ever known. I couldn't figure out what had gone wrong, no matter how I tried. Did he blame me for losing the baby?

Did he hate me for being a failure? I didn't feel a single bit of love coming off him, just resentment so deep it was like a well with no bottom. In the middle of one of these fights, I screamed at him, "I'm sorry I lost the baby!"

"Maybe it's a good thing," he spat back. "Given how shitty our marriage is, what kind of environment would this be for a baby?"

I ran to the bathroom certain I was going to be sick. *Who is this man?* I wondered through a never-ending flood of tears. The more I tried to talk about it, to find our way back to each other, the more he pulled away. Determined to save our marriage, I read every book I could find. I turned to Bible passages and looked for any possible thing to make it better. One night, I planned a romantic date, thinking maybe if we could just be alone in a romantic setting, I could thaw some of the ice that was hardening between us.

"This is a stupid waste of money," he said distractedly, "but fine, let's do a date night because that's *really* where I want to be." He actually rolled his eyes at me as he spoke. He avoided family events, anything where we would have to be together. It seemed the more I tried, the more I talked, the more I cried, the further and further he hid away from me. It felt like we were on the very edge of losing each other permanently.

I was back to crying every day. I lost weight and hid behind a fake smile plastered on for Brexton, family, and friends. I made excuses for Kyle's absences that were getting harder and harder for people to believe. I started to get wind of rumors swirling through the NASCAR circuit that we were having marital problems. We were an avalanche, gaining speed as we plummeted downhill to a divorce. In a last-ditch attempt to stop that from happening, I asked Kyle to go to marriage counseling, expecting to be mocked or ignored.

To my surprise, he agreed.

I wish I could say it was a magic bullet, and after a few gentle conversations guided by a professional we were back to our old loving selves, but it was hard. There were many painful hours in the office, exploring hurts deeper and more surprising than either of us expected. At first, things got worse. Every new session was like ripping scars off wounds so old we had both forgotten they even existed. Every nerve was exposed and every vulnerability exploited. Those months were some of the loneliest of my life, and they kept getting worse as we dug into the work. But that's the thing about therapy: It *is* work, and we kept at it. Slowly, we learned how to understand each other again, and how to communicate.

We learned that grieving is a process that is different for everyone. We discovered that when grieving styles don't align, huge problems can arise. We'd spent months walking on eggshells, sometimes stepping too hard and breaking the fragile shells into sharp shards. Our therapist taught us how to talk to each other more effectively and gave us strategies to avoid eruptions. We learned to focus on the reasons why we loved each other in the first place and to see each other in that loving light that had nearly been extinguished. Our counselor taught me how to build myself anew, to become stronger and more capable. Under his guidance, I started making changes to find the best version of myself—not for Kyle, but for me. I found Elevation, a church that I love. I committed myself to prayer and went back to *Jesus Calling*, my favorite devotional. I became stronger, more confident, and closer to God. Kyle was also doing his work. He read the books, went to the sessions, and put in the time. With slow progress, we bent our separate paths back toward each other. We learned to connect again, to value and respect each other, and to love sincerely, without pretense. With a renewed commitment in our hearts, we rediscovered our faith in each other. Ultimately, we became stronger, with a deeper understanding of each other and how to communicate, but we have to keep working at it. Luckily, our family is worth the work.

30

GOOD THINGS COME IN THREES

After a year spent with each of us tearing ourselves down and helping build each other back up, reinforcing our relationship, and rediscovering our love for each other, we were happy. Our marriage was again strong. I felt strong. I learned to love myself and my body again, to stop the punishment and blame and instead focus on self-love and fulfillment, and my relationship with God was where I wanted it to be—not a fleeting prayer before bed or a meal, but a true one of gratitude and appreciation with the understanding that even in the darkest of times we are never alone.

One day, Brexton asked us if he would ever have a new little brother or sister. Kyle and I talked long into the nights, probing at the repairs in our family, making sure they were as strong as we believed. We each looked deeply inward at ourselves, making sure we wanted this. Then we each questioned the other, taking each other into consideration in a meaningful way. After much reflection, and with perfect love and perfect trust in our hearts and each other, we decided we were ready.

It's hard to overstate how different this third round of IVF felt compared to the past two. We didn't know anything the first time, so each experience was new. It was scary, but exciting, and every step felt like a leap forward to inevitable success. Our second round was easy. We'd known what to expect, shared each step with the world, and relished the opportunity to help educate others through our experience. Then we lost our daughter and everything we thought we knew along with her. So, our third round was subdued and secret, hopeful, and terrifying at the same time.

We didn't tell anyone, not even Brexton. I could still feel the loss of my miscarriage, and while my heart no longer burned with sadness or shame, her absence remained palpable. Now that I knew what that felt like, I couldn't bear to let anyone know our plans. I didn't want to make another video announcing the process and a resulting successful pregnancy only to have to announce a miscarriage scant days later. I never wanted to tumble into the depths of despair and nearly lose my marriage again.

Of course, this secrecy presented its own problems. I'm someone who prides herself on being a loud, public voice for reducing stigma around reproductive healthcare. I had to keep telling myself to take my own advice: No woman owes *anybody anything* about her pregnancy or about her attempts to get pregnant. This time, I just couldn't share. I needed to put myself and my own mental health first, but it was a constant struggle to keep guilt at bay. I also didn't want to get Brexton's hopes up again only to crush them. This was an experience we were going to hold to ourselves until we couldn't hide it anymore.

Our drive to REACH for this embryo transfer was spent without conversation, Kyle and I lost in our own thoughts. We played K-Love, the Christian radio station, for inspiration on the drive. We sat side by side in the front seat, trying to absorb God's work and reflect on His path for us. The music and the message calmed our fears, and I reached across the center console to hold Kyle's hand. It was so good to feel connected to him again, to know our hearts beat in the same rhythm. We'd endured so much, and each of us had been pushed to our breaking points. It nearly cost us our marriage, but through hard work, a lot of therapy, and faith in God and each other, we came back together closer than before. Like steel, we had been hammered and tempered into something strong and powerful.

We pulled into the clinic and paused for a final moment of reflection in the car before heading in. Kyle squeezed my hand, and I looked deeply into his eyes. Neither of us spoke, we just looked, each of us allowing the other space to process their feelings and prepare for what was to come. Finally, I nodded slowly. "I love you," he said to me, and we stepped out of the car. I was anxious, unsure what to feel. I had two polar opposite points of reference: Brexton and the daughter we lost—heaven and hell—and there was no way to know which path we were taking on this day.

There were no words to describe how badly I wanted this, or how terrified I was of it not working again. I tried to will my vision of the future into existence: Kyle holding his little girl, the first ringlets of chestnut hair just starting to form on her tiny head; Brexton in the hospital, kissing his baby sister hello for the first time; me, introducing my parents to their granddaughter as her warm skin pressed against mine and I breathed in the fresh scent of her for the first time. I tried to focus on these thoughts and ignore the images lurking behind them: a clot, splashing bright red on a tile floor. The anguish of being a failed vessel for another baby of mine.

Once again, we were led into the same curtained room we'd visited for each of our other transfers. Gone were the warmth and excitement from the last time. This was different, solemn. What we were about to experience was wrapped in a tornado of warring emotions, and keeping it contained took all our energies. There was nothing left for chitchat. After the nurse left for us to get changed, Kyle and I exchanged glances. He smiled at me encouragingly, and together we wordlessly reassured each other that we had this. I needed to be strong and confident, but I couldn't shake the soul-wrenching turmoil of the miscarriage completely.

I undressed, carefully folding my clothes into a neat pile on one of the gray chairs in the corner of the room. Once again, I put on the gown. I reached into the purse to grab the fuzzy purple socks, the hair tie, and the baby figurine that were essential to this process and quickly realized I'd left them on the counter at home. I could picture them there, stacked one atop the other, right next to where I put my purse, and seethed. It was a silly mistake, and I was frustrated with myself. The blue mesh cap kept sliding down my forehead, the hair it was designed to contain spilling out beneath its loose elastic band. My feet were cold on the tile floor, and the open gown shifted uncomfortably on my shoulders. I was still trying to get all of this to settle when the nurse came in and said it was time to go.

I gave up and lay back on the gurney as Kyle put on his own zip-up coverall and matching blue cap. I tried to take a deep breath and put the fears aside. I prayed as they rolled me slowly down the hall to the now-familiar procedure room. I looked around for Tyl, our embryologist who had been with us from the start, and had even worked with us on the Bundle of Joy Fund events, but he wasn't there. A woman we didn't know was filling his role today, and it was disconcerting. Nothing was going the way I had envisioned, and it heightened my anxiety. The bright light in the room left shadows in the corners that seemed menacing, giving everything too-sharp edges in the echoing space.

As if she could sense my unease, our guest embryologist handed me a picture of our baby, and where others may have just seen a few cells, I saw a future. I saw braided hair and polished nails. In each cell wall, I saw late-night talks about boy problems and Kyle teaching her to drive. I saw Brexton dancing at her wedding, and I saw her brushing her hair back off her face in just the same way I do. This was my daughter. With each moment spent staring at her picture, my anxieties melted away.

The embryologist explained that the embryo had warmed perfectly, and the cells were already beginning to divide. In fact, they could already see two distinct cell formations—one that was my daughter and one that would become her placenta. Even though they only spoke of her as an embryo, the *way* they spoke of her gave me a surge of confidence.

The nurse lifted my feet into the stirrups at the end of the table and strapped them in as all of my fear vanished. In that moment, even though we were surrounded by a medical team, it felt like it was just the two of us.

Then a nurse applied some cold gel to my exposed skin and ran a probe over my belly. An ultrasound of my uterus appeared on one of the large screens in the room. As she moved the device, she said that my uterine lining was nice and thick. This was a good sign, as it would provide a fertile landscape in which the embryo could implant. All of the pre-checks were complete, and it was time for our daughter to make the journey from outside my body to inside.

I felt Kyle's hand take mine as Dr. Wing again began his countdown. This time, I worked to stay present in the moment, watching the event in minute detail on the screen in front of me. As he said "one," there was again a rush of white. This time it was like the ball dropping on New Year's Eve in Times Square. The anticipation built right up until the event, and then Kyle and I were kissing, the room vanishing around us. Like a new year, hope and possibility bloomed out in front of us, and our hearts were lifted by the experience. With my anxiety gone, optimism ruled the day. My little girl was home.

31

HOW TO GIVE YOURSELF A SHOT

Unlike the previous two rounds of IVF, waiting the two weeks to find out if we were pregnant flew by this time. The NASCAR season was down to the championship race, and Kyle was one of four drivers competing for the season's crown. As a result, our schedules were jam-packed. After a four-day rest at home taking it easy and relaxing, we left for Miami where it would be nonstop media obligations, appearances, and practices all culminating in the final race on Sunday. As we got to the plane with our entourage—Brexton, his nanny Kelly, my parents, and two dogs—I whispered to Kyle that we had a little stowaway with us with a conspiratorial smile.

We pulled up to the hotel. Kyle went one way to start his chaotic week-end, and the rest of us were left to relax. We took in the sights and spent as much time as possible on South Beach, enjoying the hot sun and warm water. We built sandcastles on the beach as the sun set and discovered a little outdoor Italian restaurant with the most amazing fresh-caught fish and homemade pastas.

On the second night of our stay, Kyle planned to stay in the motorhome at the racetrack. He was gearing up for the Championship race and was going to do film study, extra strategy meetings with his crew chief, and get in the right mind-set to try to win another championship. That gave the rest of us another night poolside at the hotel, so win-win, right? Except after Kyle left, it dawned on me that he was my shot-giver. *No problem,* I thought. *I'm ready. In fact, I'm so ready I'm going to make a video of the whole process, teaching women how to give themselves shots.* With a satisfied smile, I popped on my lidocaine patch, took the progesterone-in-oil out a full forty-five minutes early to make sure it was nice and warm, and absently picked up the room while I planned how the video was going to go.

Well, woman plans and God laughs.

With hands that were *definitely* not shaking, I grabbed the needle, an alcohol swab, and a small square of gauze. On the coffee table, I propped my phone against a water bottle, then sat on the couch and checked to make sure I was in the shot. That accomplished, I hiked my dress all the way up to expose my butt, put on my most confident smile, and hit *Record.* "Hi, ladies, it's Samantha. Today, I'm going to show you how to give yourselves a progesterone-in-oil shot." So far, so good.

I gave them the quick rundown: "It's like a dart, just do it fast without thinking, and keep slow, steady pressure on the plunger." I even sounded like I knew what I was talking about. *This was going to be so good,* I thought to myself, with a self-congratulatory smile. I removed the lidocaine patch from my backside and swabbed the now-numb area with an alcohol wipe. Then I pulled the cap off the needle.

Uh-oh.

Its evil tip shined with sinister intent, a small droplet of oil oozing menacingly out of its stabby end. I began to sweat. But I *really* wanted this video to come out great, so I plastered on my fakest smile and said, "I'm going to do a countdown, ready? One ... two ... three!" On *three,* I pushed the needle into the skin, put slow and steady pressure on the plunger, and gave myself the most beautiful shot anyone has ever given. Or I would have, if I could just have willed my hand to move.

The red *Record* light on my phone mocked me; it was definitely in cahoots with the syringe.

"Shit! Oh, crap! I can't do this!"

But I needed to do this. My little girl, moving snugly into her new home, needed this. But what if I hit a nerve? What if I permanently injured myself? What if I went too deep, ruptured my spleen, and ended up without a spleen for the rest of my life because I did it wrong? With a huge effort, thinking of all the women I was going to help with my video, I tried again. And again. And again. At least ten times, I worked up the nerve only to fail at the last second.

Determined, I took one last stab at it. This time, I broke the skin, got the needle about half a centimeter in, and freaked the heck out. "Oh, no," I told the needle, yanking its malevolent end out of my skin. A small pool of blood began to well up out of the new hole in my butt and trickle down toward the couch cushion. I quickly grabbed the gauze, wiped it up, and turned off my camera in disgust. *This* was never going on the internet. It was clear, though, that I was not going to be able to give myself the shot. What to do?

I could wake Kyle up and make him do it. Except that was over an hour drive. I could call my mom, who spent her career as a nurse, and ask her to come up, but Kyle and I had decided we were going to surprise everyone this time. I'd already had the "you're going to be grandparents again" ornaments in my cart on Etsy just waiting for me to click *Pay.* Then I remembered! Brexton's nanny Kelly used to be some sort of emergency medical technician. Perfect! I texted her and asked if she would come up to the room quickly. I had a little favor to ask her.

When she arrived, I explained the situation. For some reason, as I talked, she started shaking her head and looking pale. When I paused for a breath, just after telling her how she would be just the right person to stab me, she interjected. "No way. Nope. Samantha, I used to give out Advil and put on Band-Aids. I've never given a shot in my life. I am the *wrong* person to do this."

I reassured her that no, *I* was the wrong person to do it, and she had so much medical experience, I knew she could pull it off. We went back and forth, giving each other compliments and saying how the other person was exactly smart and talented and brave enough to do this. Finally, we decided to watch a YouTube video, instructing people how to give shots. This would definitely calm us down, and it did, right up until the woman giving instructions started talking.

"You have to be very careful not to hit the sciatic nerve, or you could do permanent damage," she said before piercing her subject with what I am sure was a demonic glint in her eye.

"But what if I hit a nerve?" Kelly asked, her voice rising in pitch and volume as the questions tumbled out. "What if I break the needle off in your butt, and we can't get it out? What if I inject you with an air bubble and it goes into your heart and you *die*?" She eyed a spot of blood on the couch from my earlier attempt and said, "Is that *blood*? Great! After I kill you with the air bubble, the CSI people will find your blood on the couch, and I'll be in jail for *murdering you*, Samantha!" Well, she had me stumped. I never knew about the air bubble thing before, and now we were both in a panic. By this time, we'd wasted an entire hour, and it was clear that neither of us were giving me the shot.

As time was ticking away, she suggested that the hotel might have medical personnel on staff. Excited, I dialed the concierge and asked if they had anyone who could give me a shot.

"A . . . shot?" The woman on the phone sounded somewhere beyond skeptical.

"It's not weird or anything," I assured her weirdly. I told her it was a medical thing, and I just wasn't able to do it. She asked me a frantic flurry of questions. Was anyone in need of emergency medical assistance? Was anyone hurt? Was there anything illegal taking place? I replied with an emphatic NO to each inquiry. She told me to hold while she asked Security if they had anyone. I wondered why she was calling Security, and half expected them to come banging on my door, white jacket in tow, but she came back on the line a minute later. "I'm sorry," she said, "we've never had this request before and have nobody qualified to help."

Strike two; we were running out of options. Then Kelly remembered that there was a medical conference going on in the hotel. She had seen lots of people with badges in the lobby, and many of them had "MD" or "RN" after their names. "We could ask one of them," she suggested. This was the best idea I'd ever heard. She ran out into the hall, determined to find help while I stayed in the room and paced.

As soon as Kelly got into the elevator, a man with a red conference badge dangling off a pharmaceutical company's lanyard stepped in behind her. "Are you a doctor?" she asked excitedly.

He eyed her up and down, smirked, and said, "No, but for you I could pretend. Do you want to play doctor?" Oh, boy. One of those.

Luckily, a couple got on just then, both wearing badges. "A nurse," she cried out, "I love nurses." As the elevator doors closed, the creep said he could pretend to be a nurse too. The nurse's badge read "Shelly," and Kelly explained the situation. It turned out Shelly had been an emergency room nurse since 1996, and said that actually this was not nearly the weirdest thing that had been requested of her.

Back in the room, I was pacing and swearing up a storm when Kelly and Shelly bounded in. Shelly had me lie down on the bed, and I started explaining that she had to watch out for nerves and air bubbles and to use steady pressure on the plunger. She let me go on for a few moments and then politely reminded me that she had been a nurse since I was in elementary school. I shut up, and seconds later it was over. I jumped up, gave Shelly a big bear hug, and thanked her from the bottom of my heart. Shelly was the greatest.

And that's how you give yourself a shot.

32

CHAMPION

Sunday morning crept in like a whisper. The stillness of the race-track at that hour provided an unexpectedly peaceful place for quiet reflection. Steam rose in gentle billows from my coffee cup as I sat curled in the corner of the couch watching Kyle and Brexton play cars on the floor of the motorhome. I smiled listening to them mimic the sounds of engines and squealing tires, doing a fair impression of the cacophony that would be filling the air later that afternoon during the Championship race.

They kept up their race, and I indulged myself in looking back at how far we had come over the past year. The miscarriage nearly broke everything that mattered in my life. If you had asked me ten months ago if this moment would have been possible, I wouldn't have known how to answer. But I had come to realize that the tragic event had also helped make our lives so much stronger. It pushed us into doing the work we needed to do to find true happiness in our marriage and in ourselves. While I certainly wasn't happy to have miscarried, I felt a deep feeling of gratitude that because of it I'd gained a new community of sisters who have all shared the same pain. So many incredible women were in my life who I would never have otherwise known.

Brexton had come a long way too, and he was blessedly unscathed by all the turmoil the past year brought. He was excelling in his home-schooling, thriving in his interactions with other kids, and by all measures was a happy, healthy boy. He still asked about his sister during his nightly prayers but no longer with sadness. Rather, he expressed constant curiosity about what heaven was like for her. He wanted to know if she had friends and toys, and if she had favorite foods. His curiosity provided a cherished insight into the wonderful big brother he was going to be for our new addition.

As race time approached, the three of us walked down pit road. Brexton perched happily atop Kyle's shoulders, and I looked at my husband with love. I was so proud of him, not just because of his accomplishments behind the wheel, but because of who he had become as a husband and father. Just before the race, when they introduced the drivers, I heard thousands and thousands of people cheering for him and thought, *I married this man. I'm having his children. And he's the best man I could have picked.* The very ground trembled with the screaming of his fans, but their collective love for Kyle couldn't hold a candle to mine.

The race started, and I took my seat atop the pit box where I could watch the action. The cars hurtled by, tires and engines even louder than the crowd. Each lap brought a new memory of our journey. Our high points and lows circled in my head just as the cars circled the track. There were so many parallels between the 2015 season and 2019. Where the first year had us struggle through infertility and Kyle's wreck, the latter had us struggle through the miscarriage and the wreck of our marriage. Each of these struggles had forced us to dig so deeply into ourselves, and we had come out stronger. Each forced us to rebuild: 2015 physically and

2019 emotionally. We saw 2015 culminate in Kyle's first NASCAR Cup Championship, and before I knew it, Kyle had rocketed across the finish line as the 2019 champion. As we stood in Victory Lane posing for picture after picture, it felt special to share this secret with him; none of the photographers knew they were actually snapping pictures of a family of four.

After two days of celebration, we flew up to New York for Kyle's Championship media tour. This really brought home how we were at a pinnacle of our lives. We felt complete and content. The trip itself was another welcome distraction that made waiting to get the official word of our pregnancy easier to bear. While we were there, multiple people told me I was glowing. A random stranger approached me during one of Kyle's TV appearances and asked if I was pregnant because she could just sense something about me. I woke up one morning to a text from a friend telling me she had a dream I was carrying a baby girl. My boobs hurt, I got winded going up flights of stairs, and my sense of smell had kicked up into hyperdrive. This can be a blessing and a curse in New York, but it was great to pick up on the sweet aroma of roasting nuts from food carts before they even came into view.

Pregnant. I still couldn't bring myself to say the word aloud after the miscarriage. Even so, it worked its way into my heart. I believed I was pregnant, and my sense of everything being right with the world carried me through the rest of the trip.

33

RESULTING FURY

Friday, November 22, was the big day. Unlike my last two pregnancies, I didn't take the at-home test early. I had been so busy and distracted by everything going on, but even more than that I already *knew* it was going to be a positive result. Every sign, every feeling I'd ever had while newly pregnant was there again. My body was telling me the news before any blood test could. I was pregnant.

The day before, Kyle and I drove down to REACH for the blood test. We radiated optimism, and as we waited for the blood draw, the nurse and I happily gabbed about our favorite baby products. She was thirty-eight weeks pregnant, and I pictured myself nine months down the road, my belly swollen like hers, ready to welcome our little girl into our lives. It was almost a year to the day since I suffered my miscarriage, and what a year it had been. All we had been through, the work we'd put in, and the suffering we'd endured had led us to this exhilarating moment.

I was so happy that I barely even flinched when they did the blood draw; even the needle wasn't able to puncture my good mood. We practically skipped back to the car. On the drive home, my hand again drifted to my stomach, and I happily pinned one great idea after another on how to surprise Brexton with the news of his new little sister that would make him feel special and help him share in our excitement. It didn't even bother me that we had to wait a day for the official results.

I woke up Friday morning anticipating the call from REACH with the good news. Gliding through the kitchen, I hummed absently while preparing breakfast. There was a local NASCAR banquet that evening, honoring our Truck team for its achievement in its Owner's Championship that year. I laid out the special looks I'd put together for Kyle and me to wear later that evening and made sure all Brexton's favorite stuffed animals were packed for his sleepover at his grandparents' house. I was so focused on the packing that I missed the call from Leigh, one of our REACH nurses. When I finally noticed, I grabbed Kyle to call with me. We sat on the floor in our bathroom, where so many big moments had passed, and dialed.

Voicemail. Rats.

We decided to get a workout in while we waited. I changed into a sports bra, wincing as it went over my tender breasts. That accomplished, I noticed a new pimple on my chin and laughed. My face broke out when I was newly pregnant with Brexton, and this further confirmed that I was having a baby. Hopping on the treadmill, I began to move. Step after step I lost myself in the exercise and was startled when the phone rang. My hand shot out to turn off the machine, and I jumped down to grab my phone. I confirmed that it was indeed the REACH number flashing across the screen of my phone, and I answered. Kyle pressed his ear to the side of my head, making sure he could hear the news along with me.

"Hi, Samantha, it's Leigh."

She paused, and in the silence, I heard her take in a slow, deep breath. "I'm afraid I have some bad news."

Hot tears flooded my eyes, and blood rushed so loudly into my ears that I had to ask her to repeat what she said next before I could hear it. "We ran the test twice," she repeated sadly. "You're not pregnant. It didn't work. I'm so sorry."

The phone dropped from my fingers and clattered to the floor. Kyle wrapped me in his strong arms as I slid down, sobbing. I was blindsided —how could this be? How could my body have lied to me? I had to be pregnant; this was our happy ending. Slowly, behind the sadness and the disbelief, a new emotion emerged like heat from a freshly stoked fire: rage. I was furious.

Furious at my body for betraying me again. Furious that I was unable to feel like a real woman because infertility stripped that from me. Furious that another one of my baby girls was gone before I had a chance to meet her. Furious that others who don't even want children get pregnant without trying. Furious that I wouldn't get to feel my daughter grow inside me. Furious that I had endured the worst year of my life only to get slammed down again. Furious that, even though I'd made it my life's mission to help others facing infertility, I couldn't have another child. Furious at God for punishing me this way. Furious that I had let hope and excitement in, and it had been ripped away from me again, and furious that I'd lost my fairy-tale ending.

The rage burned hot inside me, and I let out a primal wail into Kyle's shoulder. We sat there for an hour, my fury building but with no outlet. The afternoon passed in a blur, with me wrestling to control my emotions. I had Brexton to look after, and we still had the banquet to attend.

The banquet—I was learning to hate these things. Again, I had to smile and nod and chat, and not let anyone know what I was feeling. Sitting at the table, my fingers clenched the tablecloth into a tight knot, my knuckles turning as white as the linen. This my body could do. It could pretend: pretend to be happy, pretend to be pregnant. It seemed like so much of my life for the past year had been spent hiding behind a mask, pretending to be okay and never quite getting there.

That night at home, I lay awake staring at the ceiling, and I prayed. And I told God *exactly* what I thought at that moment. I was angry: angry at Him, angry at the world, angry at my body. Angry that I knew I was a good mom and deserved another baby. Angry that Brexton would still be an only child. I cried as I prayed, no longer pretending. God sees it anyway. And as I vented, I turned my head to stare out the window to something I still can't explain.

It had been a cloudy, overcast night with drizzle hitting our windshield as we made our way back from Charlotte. I would have preferred raging thunderstorms and could probably have made some of my own if I put a little effort into it, but drizzle is what we got. But when I looked out the window, bright silver moonlight was shining on our cherry tree. Our *daughter's* cherry tree. In that moment I knew that our girls were in heaven, and they were safe, loved, and together. Slowly, peace entered my heart, cooling the raging fires—not extinguishing them but bringing them back to more manageable levels. I watched the tree glow for what seemed like hours until I finally drifted to sleep.

The next week, I had to go back to REACH for a recurring pregnancy loss blood draw that looked for anything that might give an indication of why we had suffered a miscarriage and now a failed cycle. Perhaps if there was an underlying reason, it could be treated. We only had one girl embryo left. One more chance. As I sat in Dr. Wing's office, wringing my hands and worrying that something dire was wrong with me, I thought back on all the times I'd been here before. The confusion and happiness, the good and the bad. This time, I was here alone as Kyle had work obligations. Being alone had me even more on edge, and the negative possibilities twisted and turned in my mind.

Dr. Wing had a folder in front of him, and he spent a minute reading the results while I waited. He looked at me with compassion and said that, unfortunately, everything checked out okay. There was no clear reason why I didn't get pregnant. It was a strange spot, being relieved that nothing is wrong but also being disappointed that we had nothing to fix. On paper, I was the perfect candidate, and I should be pregnant.

I knew where the conversation was going to lead, and I decided to rip off the Band-Aid and beat him to it. "Dr. Wing, we have one girl embryo left. If this were you and your wife, what would you do?" He didn't hesitate. "I'd do everything I could to give her the best chance of being born. And unfortunately," he paused for a moment, as if gathering courage, "your body is not giving your embryos the best chance. I would use a surrogate."

Well, that was that. It was decided. I had no tears, no emotions at all. There was nothing to feel right then. It was what it was. Cold and probably a little short, I left the clinic without thinking for an emotionless drive home.

My hand never once went to my belly.

I tried so hard to feel nothing because I was terrified of what feeling the loss had done to my marriage the last time. I knew that Kyle and I were in a much better place and had tools now we never even knew existed before, but the fear was real. I didn't know how much one woman could be expected to bear, and often found myself returning to the story of Job. He was prepared to accept the loss of all his children because it was God's will; I had lost two daughters. So, I put the mask on. I put every ounce of energy I had into being a good mom, a loving wife, and a good person. At the end of the day I'd collapse exhausted into bed, waiting for a sleep that rarely came.

I didn't know what to do. We had one last shot; it was now all or nothing. I wanted someone to lay out a perfect plan, a step-by-step guide that ended with a sister for Brexton and a perfect baby girl for Kyle and me, but there wasn't a plan. It seemed like we were now on the path to surrogacy, something I had never before even considered. I had no idea how to process this—that I would never again be pregnant. That another woman would feel the first kicks meant for me, that her breasts would grow heavy with milk as her belly became firm and round and obviously with child.

Another loss. Another thing to mourn. And one more chance for a baby girl.

34

ANOTHER NEW FRONTIER

When I told Kyle the results of the test and what Dr. Wing had said, he was great. "Well, there you have it; we have to find a surrogate." No complaints, not a blink of an eye. I was so grateful that he was open to taking this detour on our journey to having a daughter, but also envied his ability to compartmentalize and approach this without emotion. For him, it was a problem to be solved, and surrogacy was a solution. For me, it was a sticky, tangled web of emotions, thick and suffocating and impossible to escape.

On one hand, it was great to have the pressure taken off me. The anxiety and stress of being unable to get pregnant or carry a baby to term left me paralyzed with fear at the very thought of trying a fourth cycle. I couldn't imagine trying a fourth cycle with our last girl embryo and losing her. But on the other hand, I was jealous. I wanted that magic to happen inside me. I wanted to feel the fluttering of the first kicks deep inside me. I wanted to know that my heartbeat was her constant companion. I wanted to know how my baby felt when I woke up in the morning and she hung heavy in my belly. I wanted to embrace those things all over again that I'd taken for granted when I was pregnant with Brexton, naively thinking that I would do this again. It hurt that someone else would get to see the beautiful changes in her body that should have been happening to mine.

We made an appointment with a surrogacy agency that was recommended to us by REACH. The day of the appointment was rainy and cold, and the gray light matched my somber mood. This didn't feel joyous, but it did feel necessary. The small office was harshly lit and decorated with pictures of happy couples beaming with their babies. I wanted to be able to smile along at the pictures, but I just couldn't. It just didn't seem fair, and I felt like a horrible person for thinking that way. I knew how blessed we were to already have a son, and that we had the financial ability to move down another very expensive path toward a baby. But it still felt unfair. I hated that we had taken so long to get here, and now Brexton would be several years older than his sister. Both Kyle and I have a seven-year separation from our siblings, and we'd wanted less space between our children, yet here we were with an almost five-year-old son.

I sat next to Kyle as he flipped through brochures, feeling selfish and angry at myself as we waited. Before long, we were called back to meet with a surrogacy attorney. A powerful memory struck me of the first time Kyle and I had walked into REACH almost six years earlier. I remembered sitting there wide-eyed as IVF was explained to us. That day, I had no clue how much that process would change our lives. I wondered if we were in a similar position today, about to take a step into a world that would mold us in ways we couldn't possibly imagine.

After a brief overview of the process, Kyle and I had a lot of questions. We wanted to know how we would be matched, what medical and legal procedures would be required of us, each answer seeming only to spark more questions. But the most pressing one was, "How long?"

"Well," she said carefully, "it can be up to eight months generally. Potentially more since you're not exactly ideal candidates."

Not exactly ideal candidates? What did that mean? "But we're a loving, successful couple. We have a great son already. How can we possibly not be an ideal candidate?" Anger flashed behind Kyle's words, and she responded quickly to clarify.

"It's not about you personally, it's that you only have one girl embryo left. Most surrogates want to have several embryos available so that if something goes wrong, they have another opportunity to collect their entire stipend. Have you considered undergoing another round of IVF to get more embryos?"

Now it was *my* turn to be angry. How dare she speak of our embryos as if they were a commodity instead of my daughter. Heatedly, I replied, "Another round of IVF is not an option. We'll be proceeding with our one embryo."

She said she understood but had to lay out all the possibilities on the table. As she assured us she would see what she could do, I sat back and seethed as I let Kyle take over the discussion of the financials. We left without making a firm commitment.

A few days later, still unsure on the best way to go about finding our surrogate, we turned to social media. The outpouring of love and support we received in response was overwhelming, much as it had been a month earlier when Kyle used his NASCAR Championship speech to discuss our infertility journey. We got a lot of feedback, and one of the better ideas was to use a surrogate a close friend or family member could vouch for, but with whom I wasn't close. This would keep it from being a big problem in our personal or family lives if things didn't work out.

It just so happened that right around the same time, such a person reached out. She was a friend's sister and had always had it in her heart to be a surrogate. She was young, healthy, and had three perfect children of her own. I was a little slow in responding because I was not at all sure how to move forward. Did it make sense to go without an agency? They managed contracts and provided some legal protections that we'd have to be very careful about. They also brought a degree of expertise and experience that would alert us to potential roadblocks we didn't even know to look for.

Ultimately, I decided that proceeding without the agency would be best. It felt less transactional and more personal. And while I very much liked this woman, I did not know her very well, and there was no potential of ruining a treasured friendship if we disagreed on the business part of it. It felt preordained, as if God took what was in my heart and manifested it in the world. We started slowly, talking via text and then meeting for dinner. The more we talked, the more right it felt. We had so many uncanny similarities. We attended the same church, although not at the same location. We had very similar outlooks on the birthing process. She and I both shared the "semigranola crunchy-type" views on giving birth, each having used a midwife but also given birth in a hospital. We even used the same brand of prenatal vitamins!

What sold me, though, was when she came up with the idea of letting me "catch" my daughter when she was born, so my hands would be the first hands to touch her. This thoughtful, kind gesture melted my heart and convinced me this was the way to go. I was in a daze of gratitude and joy, and finally understood what women who had a great surrogate were talking about when they talked about finding a new sister.

Once we'd all agreed that this was a good match, a conversation full of happy tears and hugging, we began the process with REACH. There, we discovered another coincidence—she had met with Dr. Wing several years before when they were first trying to get pregnant. Back then, she had a blocked fallopian tube, but we were confident it was no longer a problem. After all, she'd had three successful, natural pregnancies. They were thrilled to see us heading down this path together.

The only hang-up was that she still wasn't getting her period from her last pregnancy six months before, so we had to wait. Still, we took good advantage of the time and made a pregnancy plan. Our calendars aligned, and we agreed that if her monthly visitor came back soon, we would start right away. "But," she counseled, "we should stop stressing too much, pray together, and leave it in God's hands." Not *twenty-four hours later* she called me with excitement in her voice. She'd had her period!

Just a few days after, REACH brought her in for her checkup. I couldn't believe how fast it was going. Each step flowed right into the next, every potential obstacle was cleared with ease. I loved our surrogate and was so blessed to have her in our life. Just a few weeks prior I was almost convinced our dream was unattainable, and now we were sure it was about to be realized.

At least, we were sure right up until REACH called with the results of her exam.

Our surrogate's fallopian tube was still blocked. "Okay," I told the nurse on the other end of the line, "but that shouldn't matter, right? I mean, she's had three babies of her own, and we don't even need her fallopian tube. We're using our embryo; her eggs have nothing to do with it."

Well, her eggs may have had nothing to do with it, but her fallopian tubes apparently did. Fluid might leak from the blocked tube, making success less likely and infection more. We couldn't move forward without her having surgery to remove the tube. Once again, just when things were going their best, the rug was ripped out from under us. She was a mother of three, one of whom was just a baby. I couldn't ask her to do the surgery—the downtime would be too much for her to manage, and if anything happened to her during surgery, I would never be able to live with myself. We had to say goodbye to the idea of the perfect surrogate, and it felt like saying goodbye to the idea of my baby girl yet again.

Crushed, I sent a dejected email to the surrogacy agency. We paid the fee, signed the required agreements, and started that process. It's such a bizarre experience—almost like speed dating. The agency sets you up with someone who sounds great. There are butterflies; hope blossoms in your heart for someone you've never even met. And then there are the meetings—some first "dates" are almost perfect. You laugh, agree on almost everything, and feel connected, but later something keeps things from working out. There are some of these first meetings that are awkward, with no connection and no real path forward. Each encounter is an exercise in vulnerability. Asking someone whom I knew so little about personally to carry my child, such a monumental event, left me feeling exposed, exhausted, hopeful, and often crushed.

After every meeting, whether good or bad, I was flooded with gratitude to these women for their willingness to carry my child. But I was also so dejected that this was what my pregnancy journey had become. Sitting across a table from a complete stranger essentially begging them while trying not to appear desperate for them to carry my child. I was desperate to convince them that I was a worthy mother so that they would use their functioning body while my womb sat achingly empty. Even so, I knew in my heart that this was the best chance we had to get our daughter. I shoved the emotions down and forged ahead.

And that's where we stand today. Waiting, again. I wish there was a satisfying end to the story, a fairy-tale snapshot of a family of four with Brexton standing on the beach, squinting into a sunny day, holding his baby sister's hand in his. But there isn't. We have many hoops through which we still need to jump while we search for the perfect surrogate.

Long ago, when we started down this difficult and unexpected path, we were naive and optimistic. Never in my life would I have imagined how we would be tested, hammered, and forged anew. But that's how we are as people. It's hard to imagine something so arduous for ourselves until we experience it. I have knowledge that I never expected to have. I have my son, and my husband, who I love more than words can convey. I don't have my daughter. Yet.

But I also have faith. Faith will see us through this. Faith will guide us through our darkest nights, and faith will bring my family to its whole true form. I am a mother, to one beautiful boy here on earth and two girls waiting for me in heaven. And I am a fighter who will never stop fighting infertility.

Part II

ADVICE

You've read our story and seen the many obstacles we faced during this voyage that we are still on. Kyle and I handled some of them with grace and others in ways we now regret. I have had my personal strength shaken and tested to its very core, my marriage pushed right to the sharp edge of the abyss; I've lost important friendships and rebuilt others. I've discovered new friends, and also poured my heart and soul out to complete strangers over social media in bouts of deep longing for connection with women who understood my pain.

Through getting it right and getting it so very wrong, I've found answers to many questions I had at the beginning. In the following chapters, I hope to share some key lessons that I have learned over the years to help you navigate the treacherous waters you may sometimes fear are too deep to cross. I hope the information here helps provide solace and inspiration, and maybe makes your infertility fight easier than it might otherwise have been.

TAKING CARE OF YOURSELF

FINDING PEACE, REDUCING STRESS, AND STAYING HEALTHY THROUGH INFERTILITY AND LOSS

Self-care and self-love when you're dealing with infertility are so important. For me, it felt like my body had betrayed me. My mind was lost in a morass of worry, alternating between a hyperfocus on all things fertility related and the inability to focus at all. This is a common thread among the women I talk to. We've felt like we were drowning in existential despair, anxiety, and depression, desperate for a life float. I wish I had better strategies for coping, but the waters got so deep so quickly I was in trouble before I knew what was happening.

So please, believe me when I tell you this: *You deserve happiness*. You deserve to spend time focusing on yourself, and you have permission to do that without feeling guilty. Investing in healing, coping, processing, and moving forward is the best thing you can do for yourself.

Adjusting to Your New Normal

1. Don't hide or downplay your emotions to yourself.

Self-care begins with honesty. I spent so much time feeling so hurt and betrayed after the miscarriage and subsequent marital challenges that after my third failed cycle, I didn't want to feel those things anymore. I wanted to squish them as far down into myself as I could and pretend that everything was okay. Boy, was that the wrong thing to do. It only led to emotions erupting at a later time and usually pointed in the wrong direction. Give yourself the space to feel and let your emotions out.

According to family therapist Brianne Schutter, LMFT, safely acting out emotions can be freeing and purifying. Crying can be renewing. Allow yourself to be creative with your feelings. Splatter a canvas with paint, scream as loud as you need to, have a fight with a pillow and win. Manifesting your emotions physically *in a healthy way* often can help reduce their emotional impact.

2. Talk it out with a therapist or trusted confidant.

In the depths of my despair following my third-round failure, I called a therapist who specializes in fertility-related trauma: Chiemi Rajamahendran, an infertility support counselor and founder of Miss Conception Coach. She explains that you need to acknowledge you are facing a traumatic situation and that it deserves validation and attention. My feelings were still too raw at that moment for me to process them alone, but face-to-face therapy or even talking it out with a loved one seemed too intimate. I didn't want to have to look anyone in the eye or let them see my tears. I just wanted to talk over the phone and have someone acknowledge my feelings and help me work through them. If you feel like you need therapy but are in the same space I was in, teletherapy might be the answer for you. Friends and loved ones, though they do offer a great deal of love and support, are not trained professionals and might not meet your needs or expectations. They may want to help you fix the situation, but their personal love and worry for you might make that difficult for both of you.

3. Create boundaries.

Boundaries are about *your* needs. It's important to remember that *nobody* is entitled to more of you than you are willing or able to give. It's important to put your healing and needs at the front of the priority line. Be direct in your expectations and needs. Verbalize what you do and do not need in regard to conversation and physical contact. After my miscarriage, friends and family would want to come over and visit to support me. When I was ready for company, I told them that I would love for them to come over and spend time with me, but I asked them to keep conversations away from my miscarriage. I also made sure they knew that although I loved them, I really couldn't handle hugs or physical contact just then as they made me too emotional. I needed a break from all the sadness, and I learned that providing these guidelines didn't push people away; it allowed them to get as close to me as I could handle. If someone can't respect your boundaries, it's time for you to put yourself first and create distance from this person for a while.

One thing that often gets overlooked in dealing with boundaries is setting them for yourself. Get this: if you've suffered a miscarriage and you're not ready, *you don't have to go to your loved one's baby shower.* You don't have to put yourself in any position that you are not ready to handle. It is not your responsibility to set your healing back to make other people happy. Explain why to your loved one, and they'll understand. Trust me, I forced my way through myriad situations only to end up sitting alone in a bathroom crying while everyone was sipping pink punch and playing baby games. Treat anything that is a trigger for you the same way. If Facebook connects you with too many pregnant people, don't log on. Give yourself space to do something that doesn't leave scars. You are the boss of your own life.

4. Life will be different for a while. Accept it.

We live in a world where we can get anything we want instantly. Tap your phone for a few seconds, and dinner is on its way to your door. Want to know something? Ask Siri. Instant gratification is all around us, *except when it comes to our pain*. Not feeling totally healed right away is hard to accept, but you're lying to yourself if you think this process is a weekend fixer-upper. There will be good days and bad days or days that flash back and forth like a Ping-Pong match. Love yourself even when you feel unlovable. Also, know that depending on the loss you are experiencing, hormonal changes can play a major role. Chiemi also mentions, "We can't underestimate the effect that hormones play in our overall mood. Our bodies undergo an incredible amount of hormonal change each month naturally and with medication, which alters our moods drastically. Give yourself grace in how your body is reacting to things around you, and remember it will often be vast swings of highs and lows. It's normal for you not to feel 'like yourself' some days. On days you feel extra sensitive to things around you, simply nourish and soothe yourself any way you can because you truly deserve it."

5. Changes in sleep patterns.

Dealing with trauma can make a good night's sleep difficult to come by. According to Brianne Schutter, LMFT, you need to accept that interruptions in sleep are often part of the loss, and know they will only be temporary. She also recommends meditation, deep breathing exercises paired with focused muscle relaxing, or quiet music when you are experiencing a loss in sleep. She says if you don't fall asleep within an hour of trying, then get up and do something for a while—read, color, journal, or listen to a sleep meditation—then try to go back to sleep. Finally, she cautions that the worst thing to do is to lie in bed letting your negative thoughts run on repeat.

6. Do not compare your situation to others.

Healing is not a contest. Your pace is your pace, not your sister's pace, or your friend's pace, or a celebrity's pace. *Your pace.* No amount of time is the correct time, and the same goes for grief. My friend Ali Prato, host of the *Infertile AF Podcast,* hears over and over again how women feel like they should be doing better because someone else seemed to recover more quickly, or that they should feel better about their situation because it is "not as bad" as what other women have endured. Every infertility path is difficult. It's not about who has had more miscarriages or failed cycles; a loss is a loss. We do ourselves a disservice by comparing ourselves to others because we invalidate our own feelings. Your trauma is real. It can be the loss of a baby that could have been or the loss of your dream or the loss of time. We need to be allowed to have that space to process and grieve at our own pace.

Managing Stress

1. Get lost in a good book.

A good whodunit is the perfect way for me to let my brain escape my troubles. For you, it might be a romance or a sci-fi journey to another world. Anything that hooks you? Read as much of it as you can.

2. Journaling.

Years ago, long before I was ready to tell anyone that we were struggling to get pregnant, I wrote down my frustrations, my hopes and dreams, and positive quotes, or just vented—expressing everything pent up in me on paper was so satisfying. Brianne Schutter, LMFT, also notes that writing takes the power of the emotion from feeling overwhelmingly inward to something outside your body, which can help you manage the feelings you're struggling with. There are no rules, so don't put any pressure on yourself.

3. Exercise.

Find an activity you enjoy and that doesn't put additional stress on you. See what calls to you and brings you happiness. Make sure you know yourself here. For some people, an intense workout can also bring intense feelings to the forefront. Start with a gentle walk, out in nature if you can swing it.

4. Take shortcuts in your life for a while.

You have faced something difficult, and your body and mind are feeling the effects. It's okay to pick the easier option for a bit. Do you always cook dinner at home? Allow yourself to indulge in takeout. Let the laundry go for a little bit, or go an extra day with dry shampoo. If cutting these small corners makes it easier for you to get through the day and keep moving forward, it's okay to take the small things off your plate for a bit.

5. Relax.

You *can* find a little space to unwind in your day. Maybe treat yourself to a special bath bomb and face mask and take a relaxing soak. Stream your favorite music from high school and dance around the living room. Treat yourself to trying a new restaurant or a floral arranging class, a book group, an extra cup of coffee out on the porch in the early morning, or anything that helps you unwind for just a few minutes. Find something that speaks to you.

Coping with a Failed Cycle

Going through IVF is an extremely complicated path because it does many things to your psyche. Perhaps most confusing is that it lets in hope that was previously missing, and it lets it in hard. Receiving a diagnosis, starting fertility medications, finding a fertility clinic, and starting IVF— each step allows a little hope to seep further in. And when it doesn't work? All that hope, all that sweet optimism collapses away from you.

I guess what I'm trying to say is to measure your hope early and get help when it doesn't work out. Try throughout the process, no matter how hard it can be, to temper your expectations. Allow yourself to be happy, but don't allow yourself to be certain. This is an uncertain world, and pregnancy is one of the least certain parts of it.

Finding Closure for a Miscarriage

Finding closure is difficult because you don't have anything tangible— no baby to hold or to memorize their distinct features. I guess in a way this made it harder and easier all at once. After the failed cycle, I also felt like I needed some closure, so I decided to get a small tattoo in our girls' honor. This is not the first tattoo I have for my children. Behind my ear sits a peony, Grandma's and my favorite flower. It has eight petals, one for each of the embabies, and the stem is a needle in honor of our journey. Inside the leaves is "5:18," which is Brexton's birthday and also a nod to Thessalonians 5:18: "Give thanks in all circumstances for this is God's will for you."

My other tattoo is on my right ring finger. It's a heart made out of two crosses, one for each of the girls I lost. It's the same finger where I wear my Brexton push present—a gift from Kyle for "pushing" out our baby —a delicate sapphire and diamond ring. So, in my mind and on my body, Brexton and his sisters are together with me. It brings me comfort glancing down at my hand and seeing this.

Over the years, I've come across several things women and families have done to find closure. I want to thank these women for their honesty and vulnerability in sharing these stories with me so that I could include them here for you.

Each year at a local homeless shelter, one woman anonymously sponsors a cake and gift for a child whose birthday is on or close to one of the would-be birthdays for the babies she lost. It brings her comfort and joy to see how happy this special gift makes this child and is a beautiful tribute to her babies. Another wrote that she bought herself a birthstone ring in remembrance of her lost children. It's a solitary birthstone surrounded by a gold band with angel wings, and she wears it daily to remind her of her sweet angel.

Someone who suffered seven miscarriages wrote to tell me that years later she still found herself longing for a sense of closure. So, she threw a baby shower asking for monetary donations from the guests, which she then donated to seven different charities that supported single mothers in various situations. From stars named in honor of lost babies, puppies adopted, and artwork displayed in their memory, butterflies or balloons released in a beautiful celebration of life, and new blogs listed to share their stories, each of these women related a beautiful memory of finding their way through the darkness.

Looking at Life Through a Different Lens

Everyone envisions a pregnancy as a couple making love and having this beautiful nine-month journey filled with bump pictures and baby showers. But there doesn't have to be the one perfect picture just because movies, Instagram, and even others say that this is the best way. It is time to get rid of stigma and be open to the idea of donor eggs, donor sperm, donor embryos, surrogates, adoption, or whatever it might be or take to make your dreams of becoming a family come true. The journey might not look like the fairy tale you imagined, but that doesn't mean your journey has any less value or is wrong.

It took me awhile to get to this point. I spent years painstakingly comparing myself to others and feeling like a failure. I wasted so much time coming down hard on myself and making my journey more miserable. I exhausted so much energy trying to pretend everything was happy and okay with myself, our marriage, everything so that people didn't know how crazily our world had been flipped upside down with infertility.

Well, you know what? Life is ugly and messy and disappointing, and if that's your sole focus, you'll live in a constant state of sadness and despair. If you choose to look at your situation under a new light, you will see you are perfectly imperfect, and that's exactly the best way to be because that is how God made you, and you have to trust in His way, not your own.

At Elevation Church the pastor spoke about how everyone tries to live up to this picture that we've created in our own minds. Often, it's because outside influences paint a carefully curated image of the perfect life. But those photos are filtered, photoshopped, and posed to perfection. Nobody knows what happened immediately before or after the image was taken. But God didn't make us all the same, and He did that for a reason.

There is no one correct way to make your journey to a baby. Sure, there are easier, less expensive ways than IVF, but if those weren't the cards you were dealt, then you have to persevere in finding a way that will work for you. You're a fighter, and it's okay if your story doesn't look like anyone else's.

Here's some advice I found very helpful from the clinicians at Flyleaf Counseling: Even in the waiting, find things to celebrate in your life. Do not let achievements in life be overshadowed by your infertility. Instead, take the time to honor these accomplishments like they deserve. It's time to embrace ourselves. It's time to stop hating our bodies or situations and to look at this as a life lesson. Did it strengthen your marriage? Did it make you grow as a person? Did it make you stronger? Did it make you value something more? Did you find new friends? When you stop and open your eyes to God's picture and not your own picture (or worse, someone's perfectly posed Instagram picture), you can see that even when He brings you through storms, it shapes you and makes you better. It teaches you.

It means I'll do my best to not live in sorrow and anger. I'll try to focus on the things that are blessed and good in my life instead of what is missing. During my struggles, I will choose to find joy. Through my pain, I will push through and persevere.

MANAGING RELATIONSHIPS

FINDING HEALTHY INTERACTIONS WITH LOVED ONES, FRIENDS, AND STRANGERS

Understanding Your Partner

Here are some things I know now that I wish Kyle and I understood at the start of our adventure—they would have made the entire experience easier for both of us.

1. Validate Your Partner's Emotions.

Every so often, take a moment to hit the pause button and focus on your partner's emotions. Explain to them without judgment that you want to talk to them about how they are feeling. They may not want to go there—especially if your emotional conversations typically end up in tears—but reassure them that this is a time to focus on them and not a confrontation. Sit them down and say, "I appreciate you always listening to me when I am hurt or broken by what we're going through, but I know

247

in your own ways this is hard for you too. If you want to talk about it, I'm here for you." Don't turn any of the conversation back to yourself, but instead validate their emotions and offer the support they need.

2. Have Honest Conversations.

Having difficult conversations about uncomfortable topics will let you find out where your partner might be having a hard time or discover commonalities or differences. Understanding how they feel will help you keep your relationship healthy and may give each of you new perspectives on your experience. Here are some questions to ask that will spark these conversations.

How do you feel about the failed pregnancy test?

When I asked Kyle this question, his response was that he didn't feel a personal failure each month like I did but rather extreme disappointment and hurt for me that I wanted something so badly and he couldn't give it to me. Where I let infertility permeate every single aspect of my life, he was able to compartmentalize it better: with every negative test, he'd start trying to figure out what we could do to be more prepared (if that was possible!) for the next round. His pain was more for me than for himself, but he also carried a lot of guilt for not being able to "fix" it. Hearing this helped ease a lot of tension I was feeling about our relationship. There were times when he wouldn't get upset with a failed pregnancy test, and that would take my mind to dark places. *Is he not upset because he really doesn't want a baby?* I'd wonder. *Does he not love me anymore because I can't give him a child?* It was a black hole of negativity, and understanding where he was coming from helped me find my way out.

How do you feel about our sex life?

If your experience is like mine, this is probably a huge elephant in the room, and something that's stressing both of you out. There is so much at stake when you're trying to get pregnant that it's easy to turn sex into a job.

Acknowledge this, and work on some ways to fix it. Maybe it's spontaneity on days you know you aren't ovulating, maybe it's games in the bedroom, new locations, something to take away the immense pressure that can go along with it. Most important, listen to what your partner wants, and make sex good for both of you again.

How do you feel about your diagnosis (or mine)?

Medical problems can be one of the biggest stressors in relationships. Kyle confided that since we both had issues that led to our reproductive challenges, he was able to handle his diagnosis easier. He explained that if it had just been his low sperm count that had caused us to go through IVF, it would have been harder for him to handle. Watching me go through all the pain and emotions because it was "his fault" would have been very hard to process for him, and he was actually grateful we both had issues so that he didn't have to carry the weight of it all on himself.

How do you feel about giving me my shots?

This can be truly terrifying for both partners. You basically are given a ten-minute tutorial and a grocery bag full of needles and meds, and are playing doctor at home. Try to keep the criticism to a minimum. Remember your partner isn't a doctor, and he's trying his best. Let him know that you would be scared in his position too, and help him get the resources he may need to be more confident. Remember to compliment him too for a job well done.

How are you coping with the miscarriage?

When I miscarried, of course Kyle was incredibly sad. He wanted our daughter as much as I did, but he processed it very differently than I did. For him, once the initial sadness had passed, he came to the realization that there's nothing he could have done about it and he needed to move on. This difference in how we grieved was such a huge struggle in our relationship. We didn't understand each other; we didn't have the vocabulary to even start to understand each other. It took a lot of therapy to get us back on track. Having these conversations early can help you figure out new things about your partner, and maybe help you to understand him instead of resent the way he grieves.

How do you feel when someone asks you if you are trying for a baby?

At first Kyle explained he felt off guard and didn't know what to say. As we started each round of IVF, we spent time coming up with a few statements that we felt comfortable with. The awkward feeling of not knowing what to say is stressful, and being on the same page about how much you want to divulge is something that you have to decide on as a team. Kyle and I found it helpful to have a few preplanned responses to share when someone came up against our boundaries. These ranged from "Thank you for your inquiry, but this is a private matter" to "We'll be sure to share when we choose" to "We've been trying, but want to keep that part of our lives private for right now. I'm sure you can understand how difficult it is." Planning out your responses can help you stick to your guns, short-circuit Nosey Nancys, and shut down awkward questions from people who mean well but don't know they are being hurtful.

Other Tips for Your Marriage During Infertility

1. Set a time limit.

It's important to communicate, but it's also important to get some space from everything. One of the most helpful decisions we made as we were rebuilding our marriage was setting a twenty-minute time limit on conversations around fertility and miscarriages. This made me angry at first. I wanted to go on and on about it, dwell on everything and pick it apart, over and over again. Really, though, what I was doing was adding pressure to an already explosive situation.

Ultimately, the time limit forced us to develop strategies for *effective* communication. At the start, we had to say what we needed for the conversation to work for both of us. Then we could use the twenty minutes to focus on one specific issue. For example, early on I told Kyle I didn't want him to try to offer ways to fix everything because it made me feel like things were my fault. When I told him how an OB-GYN nurse flippantly said maybe I need to drink more water to get pregnant, he understood how these small comments can unintentionally place blame. In twenty minutes, we identified a problem and provided examples of how these things existed in the real world, and we both felt heard and validated. Be careful not to be defensive when he makes suggestions or shares his needs. If he tells you he wants to have more sex or less sex, doesn't want to talk about important things before coffee, asks for Saturdays off from serious conversations, or something else that might be different from what you want, try to understand why he is asking.

2. Talk to someone else.

Seek out professional help and find support groups! Your family and friends surely want to help, but they likely don't understand what you're going through unless they have been there themselves. In our interconnected world, it's easy to find huge groups of people who are experiencing the same things you are. Seek them out. You'll be amazed at how quickly you can form connections with strangers who understand exactly what you're feeling.

Finding a therapist is so important for your mental health and your relationship. Having an objective third party whose job it is to help you can provide a safe environment for each of you to explore your emotions, but therapy is so much more than just talking about your feelings. A good therapist will help you develop strategies to short-circuit blowups, process emotions in a healthy way, and connect in a deep and meaningful way with your partner. Personally, I found a mix of individual and couples therapy was really effective. Keep in mind that you and your partner may not connect with the same therapist, and that's okay. You each have to find therapists with whom you are comfortable speaking openly.

3. Focus on why you love each other.

Take a minute to pause and focus on your relationship in ways that don't have anything to do with sex and procreation. Remember, you're trying to have a baby because you both deeply love each other—but in this fragile stage in your lives, it's very easy to lose sight of that. Here are a few things that worked for us, inspired by a collection of devotionals for spouses by Selena and Ryan Frederick: writing each other letters, telling each other five reasons why you love them, doing something together that was brand-new to both of us, re-creating one of our first dates, taking each other out to try a hobby we enjoyed individually, cooking a meal together from scratch, finding and telling each other a good joke, making love and pulling out all the stops like in the old days.

4. Hug it out.

This may sound like such an easy thing, but we sometimes forget the power of a good hug. When sex just leads you to think about why you aren't pregnant and a kiss feels too fleeting, consider a hug. A big bear hug, one that fills up your emptiness and makes you feel secure, might be just what you need. Try not to talk in your hugs. Just be, breathing together, connected, touching along most of your bodies. This closeness, this silent, secret intimacy with no pressure and only love, can be one of the most restorative medicines in the world.

What *Not* to Say to Someone Struggling with Infertility

I used to worry about what to say to people and just took the brunt of their well-meaning but triggering comments. Now I straight-up tell them how wrong they are. Some people may think it's better to take the high road, but it's actually about being an advocate for our community and educating others. Well-meaning people say things that are really hurtful while trying to help, and if these statements trigger you, those are valid feelings. It's okay to respond and let people know how hard their comments are. Here are some of the more difficult things people said to me.

1. "Just stop trying so hard and relax and it will happen."

Remember that infertility is a medical condition. Does relaxing cure cancer or diabetes? It won't fix this, either.

2. "Did you try using a pillow under your butt after sex?"

Yep, really got this one. It's amazing that people think we're so dumb we never thought about gravity. Yes, we've tried a pillow. Thank you, Doctor.

3. "Eat lots of protein and drink water."

Listen, this might be great general life advice, but pregnancy requires a healthy sperm to fertilize a healthy egg—and not in the digestive tract. Gorging on grilled chicken and washing it down with a cold gallon of Poland Spring doesn't make that easier.

4. "My sister's cousin's neighbor can't get pregnant, so I totally understand!"

No, you don't. It's okay to not understand, and it's okay to say that. Try, "That must be really hard to go through. Is there anything I can do to help make it easier for you?"

5. "You're too skinny. Gain some weight!"

We already have insecurities about our bodies due to not being able to get pregnant. Telling us to gain or lose weight when you're not *our* doctor is just making us feel even worse about our bodies. While certain medical conditions for severely underweight women can stop menstruation and ovulation, you are almost certainly not qualified to diagnose this.

6. "You really need to lose some weight."

See previous statement, and delete your social media account. Seriously, don't tell people they need to lose weight. I guarantee you there has never been a person who needed to lose weight who thought differently. You're just making it so much worse. And again, you are almost certainly unqualified to make a medical judgment on this matter.

7. "It'll happen when you stop thinking about it."

The only thing I'm thinking now is how I don't like you anymore. Seriously, this is some of the most frustrating "advice" anyone ever gives. Thinking about getting pregnant does not prevent one from getting pregnant. You're confusing concentrating with condoms. Perhaps you should take a sex ed class.

8. "It's God's will/God only gives us what we can handle."

Oh, this one hurts. You have decided that God has singled me out for pain and suffering in such a deep way. It creates a crisis of faith for many people, driving them *away* from God. When someone has more than they can handle, don't blame it on God, and don't make them feel like God is punishing them. Instead try, "I know you are really hurting right now, and although I can't fix the situation, I can offer a few Bible verses that might bring you some comfort in these hard times."

9. "You should be grateful you have (insert nice things about their life here)."

You have nice things too. Does that mean you can't want other things? Does that mean the thing you most want in the world should be ignored the way you are casting aside our desire to get pregnant?

10. "Why don't you just adopt?"

I saved this for last because there is such a thing as adoption guilt that is placed on many of us experiencing infertility, and I want to spend some time explaining why it's so hurtful. If you've had fertility issues long enough you've almost certainly been asked, "Why don't you just adopt?" I want to say at the start that adoption is a wonderful option that does so much good in the world. It's not out of the question for us in the future, and for those who do choose adoption it is a beautiful and special thing. But it is not an answer to fertility issues for so many people. First of all, infertility is a medical issue that requires treatment, and it is *personal*. The deep emotional, psychological, evolutionary, and personal motivations behind the desire to have a child are real, and for many people they are extremely important, and they are *none of your business*.

Finding Your Tribe

It's vital to connect with other women who have been on similar journeys. Having someone who's been there acknowledge, validate, and understand the pain and the desperation that you feel is a balm for your soul. It can be such a relief to have someone who doesn't want to handle you with gloves because they're afraid you're so fragile that you'll break. Other women who have struggled with infertility know how strong you are because they are just as strong as you, and connecting with people who can give you real, practical advice from their own experiences can make your path so much easier.

One in every eight people will suffer from infertility, and when it comes to miscarriages, the number is even higher: one in four. Our community is growing by the day, and to quote my girls at the FabFertility website, it's the worst club to be in but with the best members.

I connected with people from across the world via social media, and you can too. Seek out groups on Facebook. Find communities on Instagram. Form connections on apps such as Peanut and 1in4. Connect with RESOLVE. I know it can be intimidating to step into a new circle of strangers, but they will not be strangers for long. Soon, they will be your sisters.

Barbara Collura, the president of RESOLVE, the national infertility organization, has spent years helping women form strong and supportive communities. They have online support groups and can even help you find an in-person community in your area. These groups are facilitated by volunteers who've been through what you are experiencing. Barbara shared some quotes from women who've used their groups:

"The support group was my lifeline."

"I could have never gotten through what I did without my support group."

"My group made me hang in there and go the distance, and because of their support I have a daughter today. I wouldn't have been able to do this without them."

Everybody's different, and luckily, if one way of connection doesn't work for you, there are many others. From apps, hashtags, podcasts, meetup groups, and blogs, there are so many different ways you can connect with other women. There's always space for you, and we want you as part of our tribe.

Be Your Own Best Advocate

We wasted so much precious time by failing to speak up when we should have and didn't know what to ask when we did. Many of you will be lucky to have an amazing doctor who will give you the best chance at success by checking for any underlying issues early in the process. Sadly, many others will have a doctor go by the old saying, "Give it a year," and treat infertility as a female-only problem. It's easy to blindly trust doctors or what you read on the internet, but having true knowledge is power. One of the best ways to get this is to find a community of infertility warriors. Through their stories, you are able to glean knowledge and discover things you never even considered asking about.

Be prepared with a list of questions or wants for each doctor's visit so that you have a solid plan and don't forget anything. If you want to be extra equipped, there are now at-home kits like Modern Fertility or Proov that can provide actual results to a doctor and provide *you* with vital information you can use to inspire your questions. It's also important to trust yourself. You know your body and what's normal. If something feels different or wrong, you have to speak up. Your doctor needs to know. How much sex you are having, if you are bleeding, your husband's sperm, even my favorite: vaginal mucus. All of it.

Another thing I was surprised to learn along the way is that your insurance might not require a referral to go to a fertility clinic. I always thought that your OB-GYN had to send you there, but that's not the case. A reproductive doctor told me once that if you are young and healthy, you should consider seeking a fertility specialist if, after six months of trying, you don't get pregnant. I push for women to be their own advocates.

Here are common things you should talk to your doctor about:

+ If your periods are or become irregular.
+ Your sexual habits, including if you are having timed intercourse or are taking a more casual approach.
+ If you are tracking your ovulation.
+ Side effects of medications you *or* your partner are on.
+ If you have a history of miscarriage or have had other problems with pregnancy.
+ Testing your partner for fertility problems—remember that it takes two to tango!
+ Endocrine testing. Out-of-whack hormones can have big effects on your body.
+ Anti-Müllerian hormone (AMH) and follicle stimulating hormone (FSH) levels for ovarian reserve knowledge—how much reproductive potential your ovaries have.
+ Basic fertility analysis whenever you want to get a general landscape as a woman.

I'm very lucky that once we were referred to the REACH clinic, we never left. They were compassionate and organized, with a great communication system, and we never once thought about changing clinics or doctors even when things had not gone the way we hoped. I know this is not always the case for everyone, though, so I wanted to gain some insight on what to do if you are looking for a fertility clinic, or a fertility doctor, or to change clinics. I turned to Blair Nelson, my friend and founder of FabFertility, an amazing resource for people struggling with infertility. Blair has a podcast where she connects with women who open up to her about these issues. Given her breadth of knowledge, I asked her to help shed some light.

Blair explained to me that she is getting ready to begin her fifth round of IVF. During her course of treatment, she's been to three different clinics. Blair loved her first doctor so much that when she left to take a position at another clinic, Blair followed her. Unfortunately, this new clinic left a lot to be desired. Blair found mistakes in her treatment plan, had a hard time getting a hold of the team, and had difficulties managing prescriptions and scheduling appointments. She also struggled with a lack of continuity in her care team, meeting with a new nurse at every appointment, and she really missed the rapport she built with her first team. Although she adored her doctor, she realized that this clinic was not a match for her. They decided to find a new clinic. She has found the level of care she was looking for and is happy that she made the move and wanted to share what she learned through all this.

One of Blair's best pieces of advice is to remember that the clinic—from the doctors on down—works for you. You're their customer; they are being paid handsomely for their services, and you shouldn't apologize for asking questions or wanting them to explain anything as many times as you need them to for you to be comfortable and understand what is happening. Communicate your needs and expectations with them. You want to find a true partner in this journey.

Also remember that you can always get a second opinion. If you feel like a treatment course might not be the right path, or you just want more information, this is a great tool, even if you are happy with your doctor, the clinic, and your treatment plan. And don't worry about hurting your doctor's feelings. Most will even be happy to recommend another specialist to talk to. They want you to be as comfortable with your treatment plan as they are.

Sometimes you and a doctor will have to end your relationship. Guess what? That's okay too. Of course, it's important to remember that some things are outside a doctor's control. You have to be willing to make the change if you don't feel like you are getting the level of care you need. It might be a farther drive, you might be fearful of starting all over with someone new, but you deserve to find your dream doctor and clinic.

Here are a few red flags that you should pay attention to when choosing or continuing to stay with a reproductive clinic:

+ They commonly implant multiple embryos without reason.
+ They won't give you their success rates or have not reported them to the Society for Assisted Reproductive Technology (SART).
+ They are not honest and up-front about costs you will incur.
+ They push for the most expensive treatment without a justification for ignoring other, less invasive ones.
+ They have bad communication—for scheduling, test results, and so on.
+ They don't have an on-call nurse.
+ You find mistakes or inconsistencies in your treatment plan.
+ A doctor pushes you in a direction you are not comfortable going.
+ A doctor is upset that you want a second opinion.
+ The staff seems unwilling to take the time to answer your questions.
+ You cannot find any reviews or online history on them.
+ They fail to follow American Society for Reproductive Medicine (ASRM) guidelines.

Epilogue

A LETTER TO MYSELF ON MY WEDDING DAY

Dear Samantha,

Today is going to be one of the most momentous days you will ever experience. Not only is it the start of a life with the man you love with all your heart, it is the first step on a journey that will change you in ways that you can't imagine. I wish you weren't going to have to face the extreme trials that are laid out in front of you. I wish you had the valuable knowledge I have now to navigate these challenges. I wish it was going to be easier for you than it will be. There are so many things that I wish for you, but there is one thing I know for certain: you are stronger than you know, and you can do this.

Before too long, you're going to hold your baby son in your arms. Remember that every second of pain, every doubt, every trial you face will get you ready for this moment that will take your breath away. It will make you realize the magic of motherhood and why, no matter how many times you get knocked down, you will never stop fighting. It will reinforce your faith in God. And it will be worth it, although you won't know that until you're holding him. Then, worlds of understanding and gratitude will wait in store. Hang in there; there's nothing that can compare to this wondrous feeling. And as you raise him, you will continue to question if you are doing it right, but know that you are because God gave him to you, and you are his mother.

Remember to be kind to yourself and to the people who love you. There will be days when you doubt everyone around you. You will doubt the man you are about to marry, and you will be unsure if this marriage will last. It will, and although you can't imagine loving him any more than you do today, you will. What you have now is pure and real, but what you will build is a marriage founded on strength, love, communication, and support. You will doubt your friends, not knowing if they love you enough to stick with you when you are at your lowest. The ones who matter most will, and you will discover an entire new family of powerful women. You will also doubt your faith in God, unable to understand the purpose of the dark days to come. But remember that when it is darkest, He will still light your way.

You, the person you are right now, will disappear forever. Don't be afraid. The transformation that awaits you will astonish you at its end. You will find deep, fast rivers of strength flowing through you. You will overcome challenges you can't imagine right now. Two of your daughters will arrive in heaven before you ever have the chance to hold them in your arms. It's pain beyond imagining, and you will think it might destroy you. You *will* bend, but you *will not* break. After this metamorphosis, you will emerge confident and proud and loved.

Remember to breathe. Remember that crying is not a sign of weakness. Remember to surrender control when you want to hold on tightest. Remember to practice gratitude because you have and will continue to be granted so much for which you will be profoundly grateful. And remember to keep on fighting. Because you are a *fighter*.

Love,
Samantha
May 2020

About the Author

S AMANTHA BUSCH is a wife, mother, entrepreneur, lifestyle blog-
ger, IVF advocate, philanthropist, and co-owner of a professional
race team. After marrying two-time NASCAR Cup champion Kyle Busch
in 2010, Samantha jumped headfirst into the racing world, traveling
thirty-eight weekends a year with the NASCAR circuit. During this time,
she started a lifestyle blog on the topics of fashion, beauty, fitness, and
food as a passion project to connect with female race fans and eventually
accumulated her own following.

After years of trying and failing to start a family, Samantha and Kyle
were eventually led to in vitro fertilization (IVF). Realizing the toll the
journey took on them individually and as a couple, Samantha made the
courageous decision to share her journey through her blog, hoping that
her story may help ease tensions or fears, or maybe even inspire other
couples struggling with infertility to not give up hope. Samantha never
could have imagined the response to her story. Thousands of women and
men responded with their own personal struggles and a common theme:
thank you for making it okay to talk about infertility.

In May 2015, Samantha and Kyle were blessed with the birth of their
healthy baby boy, Brexton Busch, who was conceived through IVF. Understanding the physical, emotional, and financial toll IVF takes on a couple,
Samantha and Kyle started the Samantha & Kyle Busch Bundle of Joy Fund,

a foundation dedicated to granting monetary relief to couples facing the financial barriers of infertility. As of 2020, the Bundle of Joy Fund had awarded more than sixty grants totaling upward of $750,000, which has allowed more than thirty babies to be welcomed into the world.

In January 2017, Samantha fulfilled her lifelong dream of owning her own clothing store with the launch of Murph Boutique, now known as AVANTI the Label. Supporting her personal mission to empower women, the boutique offers a collection of styles and price points for every woman, so that she may look and feel her best every single day of her life.

Samantha also briefly starred in the television show *Racing Wives* on CMT.

Today, Samantha is dedicated to raising awareness about infertility, running her lifestyle blog and clothing boutique, traveling the country to cheer her husband on at his races, and raising their son Brexton, who is also embarking on his racing career, in Charlotte, North Carolina.

WEDDING DAY

Our first dance as husband and wife on our wedding day.

LOVE

My heart was bursting with love as I stared into my husband's eyes. It was impossible for my smile to get any bigger.

Prepping shots for my egg retrieval.

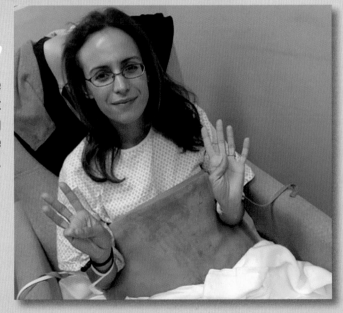

34

Still groggy from the egg retrieval, but proudly displaying how many eggs we collected.

The figurine my mom found in the dirt under a bush. Alongside is the photo of Brexton given to us on the embryo transfer day.

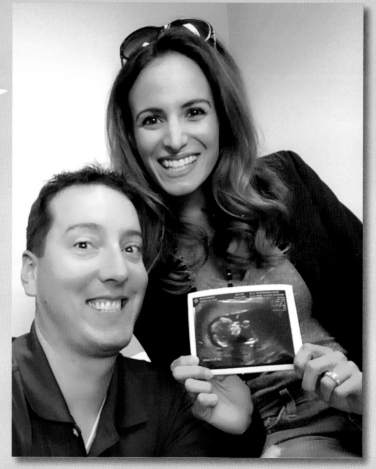

SWEET BOY

An ultrasound image of our sweet boy growing strong and healthy.

OUR BABY

Our baby announcement for Brexton.

Kissing Kyle in the hospital. Though life was turned completely upside down, he was alive and would recover. I was so grateful to God for my husband.

Loading up at the Daytona hospital to head to Charlotte for the second round of surgeries to repair Kyle's foot.

3D

Our 3D ultrasound pictures. We could not see more than Brexton's foot, but we learned a lot about his personality that day.

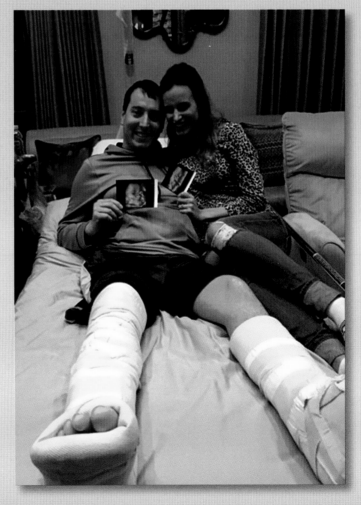

© Bailey Smith Photography

BREXTON

One of my favorite pictures from a maternity photoshoot I did while pregnant with Brexton.

JOY

The overwhelming joy and gratitude of finally having our miracle baby in our arms.

Brexton fast asleep on my chest.

Newborn photos with our sweet boy. We could not stop smiling!

VICTORY LANE

Victory Lane at the Brickyard in Indianapolis with two-month-old Brexton.

Kyle wins his first championship in 2015. After struggling with infertility and his wreck, it was a dream come true.

DREAM COME TRUE

Victory Lane in Loudon, New Hampshire.

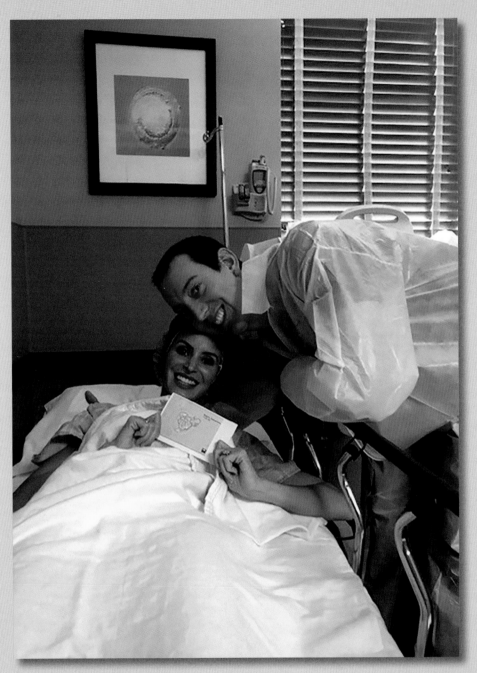

Right after our second-round transfer, holding the picture of our baby girl. *BABY GIRL*

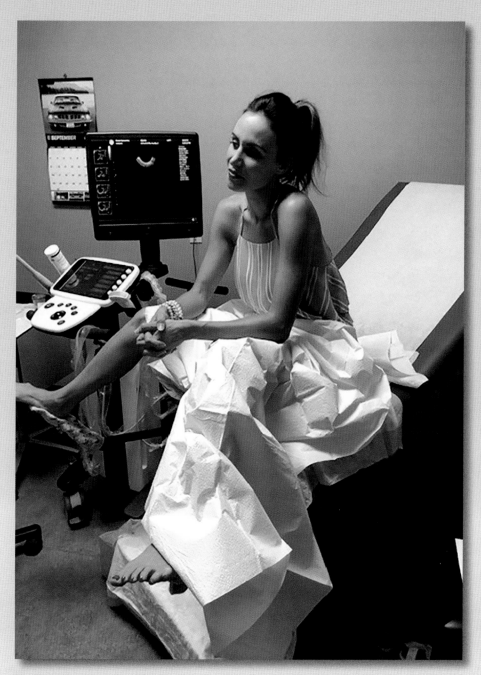

Kyle snapped this picture while we waited for an exam. We wanted to document our second round to help others facing infertility.

RED CARPET

Kyle and I were on the red carpet moments after learning about our miscarriage. We were smiling through the pain, unwilling to accept the news.

Grieving the loss of our daughter
at the tree-planting ceremony. *CEREMONY*

HAPPY

You are
my happy
place.

© Photo by Olly Yung

GRATEFUL I am grateful every day that God blessed me with being your mommy.

BUNDLE OF JOY

The Bundle of Joy Fund family. Kyle and I started the fund as a way to help alleviate the financial burden that couples face during infertility treatments.